Portfolio Risk Management!

Laurel D. Malvern

Copyright and Legal Disclaimer:

Copyright © 2024 by Laurel D. Malvern. All rights reserved.

No part of this publication may be reproduced, distributed, or transmitted in any form or by any means, including photocopying, recording, or other electronic or mechanical methods, without the prior written permission of the publisher, except in the case of brief quotations embodied in critical reviews and certain other noncommercial uses permitted by copyright law.

This book, "Portfolio Risk Management," authored by Laurel D. Malvern, aims to provide valuable insights and information on the topic of risk management within the insurance, finance, business, and money industries. While the utmost care has been taken to ensure the accuracy and reliability of the content, the author and publisher make no representations or warranties of any kind, express or implied, about the completeness, accuracy, reliability, suitability, or availability of the information, products, services, or related graphics contained within the book for any purpose.

The information presented in this book is intended for general informational purposes only and should not be considered as professional advice. Readers are encouraged to seek the advice of qualified professionals or experts in the fields of insurance, finance, and business before making any decisions or taking any actions based on the information provided in this book.

The author and publisher disclaim all liability for any loss, damage, or injury, including but not limited to indirect, consequential, or incidental damages, arising from the use of or reliance on the information presented in this book. Any reliance you place on such information is therefore strictly at your own risk.

References, resources, and links provided in this book are included for informational purposes only and do not imply endorsement or recommendation by the author or publisher. The inclusion of such references does not guarantee the accuracy, relevance, or completeness of the information contained therein.

By reading this book, you agree to indemnify and hold harmless the author and publisher from and against any and all claims, liabilities, damages, losses, or expenses, including legal fees, arising out of or in connection with your use of or reliance on the information presented in this book.

Thank you for your understanding and cooperation.

"Portfolio Risk Management"

PORTFOLIO RISK MANAGEMENT! 8

Chapter: Foundations of Risk Management 10

Chapter: Types of Risks 11

Chapter: Market Risk 14

Chapter: Credit Risk 16

Chapter: Liquidity Risk 19

Chapter: Operational Risk 22

Chapter: Other Types of Risks 25

Chapter: Geopolitical Risk 28

Chapter: Regulatory Risk 31

Chapter: Environmental Risk 35

Chapter: Cybersecurity Risk 39

Chapter: Pandemic Risk 43

Chapter: Beyond Traditional Risks: Navigating Additional Risks in Investment Portfolios 47

Chapter: The Role of Risk Tolerance and Risk Appetite in Portfolio Construction 50

Chapter: Historical Perspectives on Risk Management in Finance and Insurance Industries 54

Chapter: Principles of Portfolio Management: Overview of Portfolio Theory and Diversification 58

Chapter: Asset Allocation Strategies for Managing Risk and Return 62

Chapter: Modern Portfolio Management Techniques: Mean-Variance Analysis and the Capital Asset Pricing Model (CAPM) 66

Chapter: Incorporating Alternative Investments and Derivatives into Portfolios 70

Chapter: Risk Assessment and Measurement: Quantitative Methods for Measuring and Assessing Portfolio Risk 74

Chapter: Value at Risk (VaR) and Other Risk Metrics 77

Chapter: Stress Testing and Scenario Analysis for Evaluating Portfolio Resilience 80

Chapter: The Importance of Robust Risk Modeling and Data Analytics 83

Chapter: Risk Management in the Insurance Industry: Understanding the Unique Risks Faced by Insurance Companies 87

Chapter: Actuarial Principles and Methodologies for Risk Assessment 91

Chapter: Reinsurance Strategies to Manage Catastrophic Risk 95

Chapter: Regulatory Considerations and Solvency Requirements for Insurers 99

Chapter: Risk Management in the Finance Industry: Risk Management Practices in Banking and Financial Institutions 103

Chapter: Credit Risk Assessment and Mitigation Techniques 109

Chapter: Market Risk Management in Trading and Investment Activities 113

Chapter: Operational Risk Management and Compliance Frameworks 117

Chapter: Financial Risk Management: Overview and Objectives 122

Chapter: Hedging Strategies for Managing Currency Risk, Interest Rate Risk, and Commodity Price Risk 126

Chapter: Effective Risk Management Practices in Real-World Scenarios 134

Chapter: Integrated Risk Management: The Importance of Integration Across an Organization 138

Chapter: Enterprise Risk Management (ERM) Frameworks and Best Practices 142

Chapter: Role of Technology and Data Analytics in Enhancing Risk Management Capabilities 146

Chapter: Building a Culture of Risk-Awareness and Resilience 150

FINAL THOUGHTS 153

PORTFOLIO RISK MANAGEMENT!

In today's dynamic and interconnected global economy, the importance of effective portfolio risk management cannot be overstated. From multinational corporations to individual investors, understanding, assessing, and mitigating risks is essential for achieving financial success and resilience. In this chapter, we embark on a journey to explore the intricacies of portfolio risk management, guided by the expertise of renowned author Laurel D. Malvern.

"Portfolio Risk Management" serves as a comprehensive guide, offering insights and strategies tailored to various industries, with a particular emphasis on insurance, finance, and financial risk management. Whether you're a seasoned professional or a newcomer to the world of investing, this book equips you with the knowledge and tools necessary to navigate the complexities of risk in your investment portfolios.

Throughout this chapter and the book as a whole, we will delve into the foundational principles of risk management, explore advanced techniques for assessing and measuring risk, and discuss innovative strategies for mitigating potential threats to your portfolio's performance. By the end of this chapter, you will have a clear understanding of the importance of portfolio risk management and how it can empower you to make informed decisions and achieve your financial goals.

Join us as we embark on this journey to unlock the secrets of portfolio risk management and pave the way for a more secure and prosperous future. With Laurel D. Malvern as your guide, you'll gain the confidence and expertise needed to navigate the complexities of risk in today's ever-changing economic landscape.

Chapter: Foundations of Risk Management

Risk – a small word with immense implications. In the world of portfolio management, understanding risk and its significance is paramount to success. Welcome to the chapter where we lay the groundwork for effective risk management, exploring its intricacies and importance in shaping investment decisions.

Risk is an inherent aspect of any investment endeavor, stemming from the uncertainty and unpredictability of financial markets. Yet, it is not something to be feared but rather understood and managed strategically. In this chapter, we embark on a journey to unravel the complexities of risk and its role in portfolio management.

From market volatility to credit defaults, various forms of risk can impact investment portfolios. By gaining a deeper understanding of these risks and their implications, investors can make more informed decisions, optimizing returns while mitigating potential losses. This chapter serves as the bedrock upon which we build our understanding of risk management, laying the foundation for the strategies and techniques to come.

Join us as we delve into the fascinating world of risk management, exploring its nuances and uncovering the tools and approaches necessary to navigate the uncertainties of the financial markets. With a solid understanding of the foundations of risk management, you'll be well-equipped to tackle the challenges and opportunities that lie ahead in your investment journey.

Chapter: Types of Risks

Risk comes in many forms, each with its own unique characteristics and implications for portfolio management. In this chapter, we explore the diverse array of risks that investors may encounter, ranging from market volatility to operational challenges. By understanding these risks, investors can better prepare themselves to navigate the complexities of the financial markets and protect their investments.

Market Risk:

Market risk, also known as systematic risk, refers to the possibility of losses arising from changes in market factors such as interest rates, exchange rates, and stock prices. It is inherent in all investments and cannot be diversified away. Investors must carefully assess their exposure to market risk and implement strategies to hedge against potential losses.

Credit Risk:

Credit risk arises from the possibility of a borrower failing to fulfill their contractual obligations, resulting in financial losses for the lender. This risk is prevalent in fixed-income investments such as bonds and loans, where the borrower's creditworthiness plays a crucial role in determining the investment's return. Effective credit risk management involves thorough credit analysis and diversification of credit exposures.

Liquidity Risk:

Liquidity risk pertains to the ease with which an investment can be bought or sold in the market without significantly impacting its price. Illiquid investments may expose investors to the risk of being unable to liquidate their holdings quickly or at a favorable price, particularly during times of market stress. Managing liquidity risk involves maintaining a balanced portfolio of liquid and illiquid assets and monitoring market conditions closely.

Operational Risk:

Operational risk encompasses the potential for losses arising from internal processes, systems, or human error within an organization. This includes risks related to technology failures, fraud, compliance breaches, and other operational inefficiencies. Effective operational risk management involves implementing robust internal controls, conducting regular audits, and fostering a culture of risk awareness within the organization.

Other Types of Risks:

In addition to market, credit, liquidity, and operational risks, investors may also encounter a range of other risks, including geopolitical risk, regulatory risk, and environmental risk, among others. Each of these risks poses its own set of challenges and requires a tailored approach to mitigation.

Conclusion:

Understanding the various types of risks that investors may face is essential for effective portfolio management. By identifying, assessing, and mitigating these risks, investors can protect their investments and enhance their chances of achieving their financial goals. In the chapters to come, we will delve deeper into the strategies and techniques for managing each type of risk, providing readers with the knowledge and tools necessary to navigate the complexities of the financial markets with confidence.

Chapter: Market Risk

In the world of investment, market risk stands as one of the most fundamental and pervasive risks faced by investors. Also known as systematic risk or undiversifiable risk, it is inherent to the broader market and affects all investments to some degree. Understanding market risk is essential for effective portfolio management, as it influences the overall performance and volatility of investment portfolios.

Defining Market Risk:

Market risk refers to the potential for losses arising from fluctuations in market factors such as interest rates, exchange rates, commodity prices, and stock prices. These fluctuations are driven by a multitude of factors, including economic conditions, geopolitical events, and investor sentiment. Market risk impacts virtually all asset classes, from stocks and bonds to derivatives and alternative investments.

Types of Market Risk:

Equity Risk: Equity risk arises from fluctuations in stock prices. Factors such as changes in company earnings, industry trends, and investor sentiment can all influence stock prices, exposing investors to the risk of losses in equity investments.

Interest Rate Risk: Interest rate risk stems from changes in interest rates, particularly for fixed-income securities such as bonds. When interest rates rise, bond prices typically fall, leading to capital losses for bondholders. Conversely, falling interest rates can result in capital gains but may reduce future income from reinvested coupon payments.

Currency Risk: Currency risk, also known as exchange rate risk, arises from fluctuations in exchange rates between different currencies. Investors with international investments or exposure to foreign currencies may experience gains or losses as a result of currency movements.

Commodity Risk: Commodity risk refers to the volatility in prices of commodities such as oil, gold, and agricultural products. Factors such as supply and demand dynamics, geopolitical tensions, and weather conditions can impact commodity prices, exposing investors to price fluctuations and potential losses.

Managing Market Risk:

While market risk cannot be eliminated entirely, investors can employ various strategies to manage and mitigate its impact on their portfolios. Diversification, hedging, and asset allocation are commonly used techniques to reduce exposure to market risk. Additionally, derivatives such as options and futures contracts can be used to hedge against specific market risks, providing investors with greater flexibility and risk management capabilities.

Conclusion:

Market risk is an inherent aspect of investing, and understanding its nuances is essential for effective portfolio management. By recognizing the different types of market risk and implementing appropriate risk management strategies, investors can navigate the complexities of the financial markets with confidence and enhance their chances of achieving their investment objectives. In the chapters to come, we will explore additional risk management techniques and delve deeper into the intricacies of portfolio risk management.

Chapter: Credit Risk

Credit risk is a fundamental consideration in the realm of finance and investment. It is the risk that a borrower may default on their financial obligations, resulting in financial losses for the lender or investor. Understanding credit risk is crucial for investors, particularly those involved in lending activities or investing in fixed-income securities such as bonds. In this chapter, we explore the intricacies of credit risk and discuss strategies for managing and mitigating its impact on investment portfolios.

Defining Credit Risk:

Credit risk, also known as default risk, is the risk of financial loss arising from the failure of a borrower to repay their debt obligations in accordance with the terms of the loan or bond agreement. This risk can manifest in various forms, including outright default, late payments, or downgrades in credit quality. Credit risk is prevalent across all sectors of the economy, from individuals and corporations to governments and financial institutions.

Types of Credit Risk:

Individual Credit Risk: Individual credit risk pertains to the creditworthiness of individual borrowers or counterparties. It considers factors such as the borrower's credit history, income, assets, and liabilities. Lenders assess individual credit risk through credit scoring models and financial analysis to determine the likelihood of default.

Counterparty Credit Risk: Counterparty credit risk arises in financial transactions where one party is reliant on the performance of another party. This risk is particularly relevant in derivatives trading, where counterparties may fail to fulfill their contractual obligations, leading to financial losses for the other party.

Sovereign Credit Risk: Sovereign credit risk refers to the risk of default by national governments on their sovereign debt obligations. Factors such as economic instability, political turmoil, and fiscal mismanagement can impact a country's creditworthiness and increase the likelihood of sovereign default.

Managing Credit Risk:

Effective credit risk management involves a combination of preventive measures, monitoring mechanisms, and risk mitigation strategies. Lenders and investors can employ various techniques to manage credit risk, including:

Conducting thorough credit analysis and due diligence on borrowers or counterparties.
Diversifying credit exposures across a range of borrowers, industries, and geographic regions.
Implementing credit risk mitigation tools such as collateral, guarantees, and credit derivatives.

Monitoring credit portfolios regularly to identify emerging risks and take timely corrective actions.

Conclusion:

Credit risk is a pervasive aspect of financial markets, and its management is essential for maintaining the stability and profitability of investment portfolios. By understanding the different types of credit risk and implementing robust risk management practices, investors can minimize their exposure to credit-related losses and enhance their overall portfolio resilience. In the chapters to come, we will delve deeper into the intricacies of credit risk management and explore advanced techniques for mitigating credit risk effectively.

Chapter: Liquidity Risk

Liquidity risk is a critical consideration in the world of finance and investment. It refers to the risk that an investor may be unable to buy or sell an asset quickly and at a reasonable price, leading to potential losses or difficulty in meeting financial obligations. Understanding liquidity risk is essential for investors, as it can impact portfolio performance, risk management, and overall financial stability. In this chapter, we delve into the nuances of liquidity risk and discuss strategies for managing and mitigating its impact on investment portfolios.

Defining Liquidity Risk:

Liquidity risk arises from the imbalance between the supply and demand for an asset in the market. It can manifest in various forms, including market liquidity risk and funding liquidity risk. Market liquidity risk refers to the inability to buy or sell an asset due to limited trading activity or market depth. Funding liquidity risk, on the other hand, pertains to the inability to obtain funding or liquidity to meet financial obligations.

Types of Liquidity Risk:

Asset Liquidity Risk: Asset liquidity risk arises when an investor holds assets that are difficult to buy or sell in the market without significantly impacting their price. This risk is particularly prevalent in thinly traded securities or illiquid markets, where there may be limited liquidity providers or trading volumes.

Funding Liquidity Risk: Funding liquidity risk relates to the availability of funds or liquidity to meet financial obligations as they come due. It can occur when investors are unable to access funding sources or raise capital quickly, leading to liquidity shortages and potential default on obligations.

Market Liquidity Risk: Market liquidity risk refers to the risk of being unable to buy or sell an asset quickly and at a reasonable price due to adverse market conditions or disruptions. Factors such as market volatility, economic uncertainty, and regulatory changes can impact market liquidity and increase the risk of illiquidity for investors.

Managing Liquidity Risk:

Effective liquidity risk management involves implementing proactive measures to ensure sufficient liquidity to meet financial obligations and capitalize on investment opportunities. Strategies for managing liquidity risk include:

Maintaining adequate cash reserves or liquid assets to cover short-term funding needs.
Diversifying investments across a range of liquid assets and markets to enhance liquidity.
Establishing contingency plans and alternative funding sources to mitigate liquidity shortages.
Monitoring market conditions and liquidity metrics regularly to identify emerging risks and take timely corrective actions.
Conclusion:

Liquidity risk is a critical aspect of investment management, and its effective management is essential for maintaining financial stability and resilience. By understanding the different types of liquidity risk and implementing robust risk management practices, investors can enhance their ability to navigate the complexities of the financial markets and achieve their investment objectives. In the chapters to come, we will explore additional techniques for managing liquidity risk and delve deeper into the intricacies of portfolio risk management.

Chapter: Operational Risk

Operational risk is a pervasive and often underestimated risk that can have significant implications for businesses and investors. Unlike market or credit risk, which are more directly related to financial markets, operational risk arises from internal processes, systems, people, and external events. In this chapter, we delve into the complexities of operational risk, exploring its various sources, consequences, and strategies for effective management.

Defining Operational Risk:

Operational risk is the risk of loss resulting from inadequate or failed internal processes, systems, or human error, or from external events. These risks can manifest in a variety of ways, including errors, fraud, system failures, legal and regulatory compliance failures, and external events such as natural disasters or cyber-attacks. Operational risk is inherent in all business activities and can impact organizations of any size or industry.

Sources of Operational Risk:

Human Factors: Human error, misconduct, and inadequate training are common sources of operational risk. Employees may make mistakes, intentionally or unintentionally, that lead to financial losses, reputational damage, or regulatory sanctions.

Process and System Failures: Inadequate processes, systems, or controls can result in operational failures, such as processing errors, system outages, or data breaches. These failures can disrupt business operations, lead to financial losses, and damage customer trust and confidence.

External Events: External events, such as natural disasters, geopolitical events, or pandemics, can pose significant operational risks to businesses. These events may disrupt supply chains, infrastructure, or business operations, leading to financial losses or business continuity challenges.

Consequences of Operational Risk:

The consequences of operational risk can be wide-ranging and severe, impacting an organization's financial performance, reputation, and regulatory compliance. Operational failures can result in financial losses, legal and regulatory fines, damage to brand reputation, loss of customer trust, and business disruptions. In extreme cases, operational failures can even threaten the viability of an organization.

Managing Operational Risk:

Effective operational risk management involves identifying, assessing, and mitigating operational risks through a combination of preventive measures, controls, and contingency plans. Strategies for managing operational risk include:

Implementing robust internal controls, processes, and systems to prevent and detect operational failures.
Conducting regular risk assessments and audits to identify and prioritize operational risks.
Providing comprehensive training and ongoing education to employees to mitigate human error and misconduct.

Establishing business continuity and disaster recovery plans to mitigate the impact of external events.
Monitoring key risk indicators and incidents to identify emerging risks and take timely corrective actions.
Conclusion:

Operational risk is a complex and multifaceted risk that requires careful attention and proactive management. By understanding the sources, consequences, and strategies for managing operational risk, organizations can enhance their resilience and protect themselves against potential losses and disruptions. In the chapters to come, we will explore additional techniques for managing operational risk and delve deeper into the intricacies of portfolio risk management.

Chapter: Other Types of Risks

In addition to market, credit, liquidity, and operational risks, investors may encounter a variety of other risks that can impact investment portfolios. These risks, while diverse in nature, share the potential to influence portfolio performance and require careful consideration in risk management strategies. In this chapter, we explore some of the additional types of risks that investors may face and discuss approaches for effectively managing them.

Geopolitical Risk:

Geopolitical risk refers to the potential for political instability, conflicts, or geopolitical events to impact investment markets and assets. Factors such as trade disputes, military conflicts, regulatory changes, and changes in government policies can all contribute to geopolitical risk. Investors may experience heightened market volatility, currency fluctuations, and uncertainty in regions or countries affected by geopolitical tensions.

Regulatory Risk:

Regulatory risk arises from changes in laws, regulations, or government policies that affect investment markets and assets. Regulatory changes can impact industries, businesses, and investment strategies, leading to compliance challenges, increased costs, or changes in market dynamics. Investors must stay informed about regulatory developments and adapt their investment strategies accordingly to mitigate regulatory risk.

Environmental Risk:

Environmental risk relates to the potential for environmental factors such as climate change, natural disasters, and environmental regulations to impact investment portfolios. Climate-related events such as hurricanes, wildfires, and floods can cause physical damage to assets and disrupt business operations, leading to financial losses. Additionally, regulatory efforts to address climate change and environmental sustainability can affect industries and businesses, influencing investment decisions and performance.

Cybersecurity Risk:

Cybersecurity risk refers to the potential for cyber-attacks, data breaches, and IT security incidents to impact investment portfolios and organizations. With the increasing reliance on technology and digital infrastructure, cybersecurity threats have become a significant concern for investors and businesses alike. Cyber-attacks can result in financial losses, reputational damage, regulatory fines, and legal liabilities, highlighting the importance of robust cybersecurity measures and risk management practices.

Pandemic Risk:

Pandemic risk pertains to the potential for widespread infectious diseases, such as the COVID-19 pandemic, to disrupt economies, industries, and financial markets. Pandemics can lead to supply chain disruptions, business closures, market volatility, and economic recession, impacting investment portfolios and asset values. Investors must consider the potential impact of pandemics on their investment strategies and incorporate contingency plans to mitigate pandemic risk.

Conclusion:

In addition to market, credit, liquidity, and operational risks, investors may encounter a variety of other risks that can influence investment portfolios. Geopolitical risk, regulatory risk, environmental risk, cybersecurity risk, and pandemic risk are just a few examples of the additional risks that investors must consider in their risk management strategies. By understanding the nature of these risks and implementing appropriate risk management practices, investors can enhance their ability to navigate the complexities of the financial markets and achieve their investment objectives. In the chapters to come, we will explore advanced techniques for managing these and other types of risks and delve deeper into the intricacies of portfolio risk management.

Chapter: Geopolitical Risk

Geopolitical risk is a significant consideration for investors, as it encompasses a wide range of factors that can impact investment markets and assets. From political instability and conflicts to regulatory changes and trade disputes, geopolitical events have the potential to create uncertainty and volatility in the financial markets. In this chapter, we explore the nature of geopolitical risk, its sources, and its implications for investment portfolios.

Understanding Geopolitical Risk:

Geopolitical risk refers to the risk of political instability, conflicts, or geopolitical events affecting investment markets and assets. These events can have far-reaching consequences, ranging from economic sanctions and trade disruptions to military conflicts and regime changes. Geopolitical risk is often unpredictable and can lead to heightened market volatility, currency fluctuations, and uncertainty among investors.

Sources of Geopolitical Risk:

Several factors contribute to geopolitical risk, including:

Political Instability: Political instability in countries or regions can create uncertainty and volatility in the financial markets. Factors such as government corruption, civil unrest, and regime changes can impact investor confidence and lead to capital flight.

Military Conflicts: Military conflicts, wars, and terrorist attacks can disrupt economies, infrastructure, and business operations, leading to financial losses for investors. Heightened geopolitical tensions can increase the risk of military escalation and have widespread implications for global security and stability.

Trade Disputes: Trade disputes between countries or regions can result in tariffs, import/export restrictions, and trade barriers, affecting international trade flows and supply chains. Trade tensions can lead to market uncertainty, currency fluctuations, and reduced investor confidence.

Regulatory Changes: Changes in government policies, regulations, or laws can impact industries, businesses, and investment markets. Regulatory reforms, tax changes, and policy shifts can create uncertainty for investors and affect the profitability of investments.

Implications for Investment Portfolios:

Geopolitical risk can have significant implications for investment portfolios, including:

Heightened Market Volatility: Geopolitical events can lead to increased market volatility and uncertainty, making it challenging for investors to predict market movements and adjust their investment strategies accordingly.

Currency Fluctuations: Geopolitical tensions can impact currency exchange rates, leading to currency fluctuations and affecting the value of international investments and foreign exchange exposure.

Sector and Regional Impact: Geopolitical events may disproportionately affect certain sectors or regions, leading to sectoral or regional market movements and impacting investment returns.

Conclusion:

Geopolitical risk is a complex and multifaceted risk that requires careful consideration in investment decision-making. By understanding the sources and implications of geopolitical risk, investors can better assess their exposure and implement risk management strategies to mitigate its impact on their investment portfolios. In the chapters to come, we will explore advanced techniques for managing geopolitical risk and delve deeper into the intricacies of portfolio risk management.

Chapter: Regulatory Risk

Regulatory risk is a critical consideration for investors operating in today's dynamic and heavily regulated financial markets. It encompasses the potential impact of changes in laws, regulations, or government policies on investment markets and assets. Regulatory developments can have far-reaching implications, affecting industries, businesses, and investment strategies. In this chapter, we explore the nature of regulatory risk, its sources, and strategies for effectively managing it.

Understanding Regulatory Risk:

Regulatory risk arises from changes in laws, regulations, or government policies that affect investment markets and assets. These changes can result from shifts in political priorities, economic conditions, or societal trends, and can impact various aspects of the investment landscape. Regulatory risk can manifest in different forms, including compliance challenges, increased costs, or changes in market dynamics, and requires careful consideration by investors.

Sources of Regulatory Risk:

Several factors contribute to regulatory risk, including:

Legislative Changes: Legislative changes enacted by governments can impact industries, businesses, and investment markets. Changes in tax laws, financial regulations, or securities legislation can affect market participants and investment strategies.

Regulatory Reforms: Regulatory agencies may implement reforms or amendments to existing regulations to address emerging risks or market developments. Regulatory changes such as Basel III in banking or MiFID II in financial markets can have significant implications for market participants.

Policy Shifts: Changes in government policies or priorities can influence regulatory agendas and impact industries and businesses. Policy shifts related to environmental protection, consumer rights, or economic stimulus programs can affect market dynamics and investor sentiment.

Implications for Investment Portfolios:

Regulatory risk can have several implications for investment portfolios, including:

Compliance Challenges: Regulatory changes may require investors to comply with new reporting requirements, disclosure obligations, or compliance standards, leading to increased administrative burdens and compliance costs.

Increased Costs: Regulatory reforms may result in higher compliance costs, capital requirements, or operational expenses for businesses and financial institutions, potentially affecting profitability and investment returns.

Changes in Market Dynamics: Regulatory changes can alter market structures, trading practices, or investor behavior, leading to changes in market liquidity, volatility, or asset valuations.

Strategies for Managing Regulatory Risk:

Effective management of regulatory risk involves staying informed about regulatory developments and adapting investment strategies accordingly. Strategies for managing regulatory risk include:

Conducting Regulatory Due Diligence: Investors should conduct thorough due diligence to assess regulatory risks associated with investment opportunities, including regulatory compliance, legal risks, and regulatory enforcement actions.

Monitoring Regulatory Developments: Investors should stay informed about regulatory developments, legislative changes, and policy shifts that may impact investment markets and assets. Regular monitoring of regulatory news, industry publications, and regulatory agency announcements can help investors anticipate regulatory changes and adjust their investment strategies accordingly.

Diversifying Investment Portfolios: Diversification across asset classes, sectors, and regions can help investors mitigate the impact of regulatory changes on their investment portfolios. By spreading investments across a range of assets, investors can reduce concentration risk and exposure to specific regulatory risks.

Conclusion:

Regulatory risk is a significant consideration for investors operating in today's complex and heavily regulated financial markets. By understanding the sources and implications of regulatory risk and implementing effective risk management strategies, investors can navigate regulatory challenges and protect their investment portfolios. In the chapters to come, we will explore advanced techniques for managing regulatory risk and delve deeper into the intricacies of portfolio risk management.

Chapter: Environmental Risk

Environmental risk poses a significant threat to investment portfolios, as it encompasses a wide range of environmental factors that can impact businesses, industries, and economies. From climate change-related events to regulatory efforts aimed at addressing environmental sustainability, environmental risk presents both physical and regulatory challenges for investors. In this chapter, we explore the nature of environmental risk, its sources, and strategies for effectively managing it within investment portfolios.

Understanding Environmental Risk:

Environmental risk refers to the potential for environmental factors such as climate change, natural disasters, and environmental regulations to impact investment portfolios. These risks can manifest in various forms, including physical damage to assets, business disruptions, regulatory compliance challenges, and changes in market dynamics. Environmental risk is complex and multifaceted, requiring careful consideration by investors.

Sources of Environmental Risk:

Several factors contribute to environmental risk, including:

Climate Change: Climate change poses a significant environmental risk, with rising temperatures, changing weather patterns, and more frequent extreme weather events such as hurricanes, wildfires, and floods. These events can cause physical damage to assets, disrupt supply chains, and lead to business interruptions, resulting in financial losses for investors.

Natural Disasters: Natural disasters such as earthquakes, tsunamis, and droughts can have devastating consequences for businesses, communities, and economies. These events can damage infrastructure, disrupt operations, and lead to property losses, affecting investment portfolios exposed to affected regions or industries.

Environmental Regulations: Regulatory efforts to address climate change and environmental sustainability can impact industries, businesses, and investment strategies. Environmental regulations may impose stricter emissions standards, environmental reporting requirements, or carbon pricing mechanisms, influencing investment decisions and performance.

Implications for Investment Portfolios:

Environmental risk can have several implications for investment portfolios, including:

Physical Asset Damage: Climate-related events and natural disasters can cause physical damage to assets, leading to property losses and impairments in asset values.

Business Disruptions: Environmental events such as hurricanes, wildfires, and floods can disrupt business operations, supply chains, and distribution networks, resulting in revenue losses and operational challenges for businesses.

Regulatory Compliance Costs: Environmental regulations may require businesses to invest in emissions reduction technologies, environmental monitoring systems, or renewable energy sources, increasing compliance costs and reducing profitability.

Strategies for Managing Environmental Risk:

Effective management of environmental risk involves implementing strategies to mitigate exposure and build resilience within investment portfolios. Strategies for managing environmental risk include:

Environmental Due Diligence: Conducting thorough due diligence to assess environmental risks associated with investment opportunities, including physical risks, regulatory risks, and climate-related risks.

Climate Risk Assessment: Assessing the potential impact of climate change-related events on investment portfolios, including extreme weather events, sea-level rise, and shifts in precipitation patterns.

Sustainable Investing: Incorporating environmental, social, and governance (ESG) factors into investment decision-making to identify sustainable investment opportunities and mitigate environmental risks.

Diversification: Diversifying investment portfolios across asset classes, sectors, and regions to reduce exposure to environmental risks and enhance portfolio resilience.

Conclusion:

Environmental risk poses significant challenges for investors, with climate change-related events, natural disasters, and environmental regulations all contributing to the complexity of environmental risk management. By understanding the sources and implications of environmental risk and implementing effective risk management strategies, investors can navigate environmental challenges and protect their investment portfolios. In the chapters to come, we will explore advanced techniques for managing environmental risk and delve deeper into the intricacies of portfolio risk management.

Chapter: Cybersecurity Risk

In today's digital age, cybersecurity risk has emerged as a critical concern for investors and businesses alike. With the increasing reliance on technology and digital infrastructure, cyber-attacks, data breaches, and IT security incidents have become prevalent threats that can have far-reaching implications for investment portfolios and organizations. In this chapter, we explore the nature of cybersecurity risk, its potential impact, and strategies for effectively managing it within investment portfolios.

Understanding Cybersecurity Risk:

Cybersecurity risk refers to the potential for cyber-attacks, data breaches, and IT security incidents to compromise the confidentiality, integrity, and availability of information and systems. These risks can originate from various sources, including malicious actors, insider threats, software vulnerabilities, and human error. Cybersecurity risk is pervasive and can affect businesses of all sizes and industries, making it a critical consideration for investors.

Sources of Cybersecurity Risk:

Several factors contribute to cybersecurity risk, including:

Malware and Ransomware: Malicious software such as malware and ransomware can infiltrate computer systems, networks, and devices, allowing cybercriminals to steal sensitive information, disrupt operations, or extort ransom payments.

Phishing and Social Engineering: Phishing attacks involve the use of deceptive emails, websites, or messages to trick individuals into disclosing sensitive information or downloading malicious software. Social engineering tactics exploit human psychology to manipulate individuals into divulging confidential information or performing unauthorized actions.

Insider Threats: Insider threats occur when individuals within an organization misuse their access privileges or intentionally cause harm to the organization's information systems, data, or assets. Insider threats can result from malicious intent, negligence, or compromised credentials.

Potential Impact of Cybersecurity Risk:

Cybersecurity risk can have several implications for investment portfolios and organizations, including:

Financial Losses: Cyber-attacks and data breaches can lead to financial losses stemming from theft of funds, fraudulent transactions, business disruption, and remediation costs.

Reputational Damage: Cybersecurity incidents can tarnish an organization's reputation and erode customer trust and confidence, leading to lost business opportunities and long-term damage to brand equity.

Regulatory Fines and Legal Liabilities: Organizations may face regulatory fines, penalties, and legal liabilities for non-compliance with data protection regulations or failure to safeguard sensitive information.

Operational Disruption: Cyber-attacks can disrupt business operations, disrupt supply chains, and cause downtime, leading to productivity losses and revenue impacts.

Strategies for Managing Cybersecurity Risk:

Effective management of cybersecurity risk involves implementing strategies to prevent, detect, and respond to cyber threats. Strategies for managing cybersecurity risk within investment portfolios include:

Implementing Robust Security Measures: Adopting cybersecurity best practices, such as encryption, multi-factor authentication, and intrusion detection systems, to protect information and systems from unauthorized access.

Employee Training and Awareness: Providing comprehensive cybersecurity training and awareness programs to employees to educate them about cyber threats, phishing scams, and best practices for securely handling information and using technology.

Incident Response Planning: Developing and implementing incident response plans to effectively respond to cybersecurity incidents, minimize damage, and restore operations promptly.

Regular Security Assessments: Conducting regular cybersecurity assessments, vulnerability scans, and penetration testing to identify and address security weaknesses and gaps in defenses.

Conclusion:

Cybersecurity risk is a pervasive threat that can have significant implications for investment portfolios and organizations. By understanding the nature of cybersecurity risk, its potential impact, and implementing effective risk management strategies, investors can mitigate the risk of cyber-attacks and protect their investment portfolios from financial losses, reputational damage, and regulatory scrutiny. In the chapters to come, we will explore advanced techniques for managing cybersecurity risk and delve deeper into the intricacies of portfolio risk management.

Chapter: Pandemic Risk

Pandemic risk has become a pressing concern for investors and businesses worldwide, particularly in the wake of the COVID-19 pandemic. Pandemics, characterized by the rapid spread of infectious diseases across regions and countries, can have profound implications for economies, industries, and financial markets. In this chapter, we delve into the nature of pandemic risk, its potential impact, and strategies for managing it within investment portfolios.

Understanding Pandemic Risk:

Pandemic risk refers to the potential for widespread infectious diseases, such as the COVID-19 pandemic, to disrupt economies, industries, and financial markets. These events can lead to supply chain disruptions, business closures, market volatility, and economic recession, affecting investment portfolios and asset values. Pandemic risk is characterized by uncertainty, rapid transmission rates, and the potential for severe health and economic consequences.

Sources of Pandemic Risk:

The sources of pandemic risk include:

Infectious Disease Outbreaks: Pandemic risk originates from outbreaks of infectious diseases, such as influenza, Ebola, or COVID-19, which have the potential to spread rapidly and impact populations worldwide. Factors such as globalization, urbanization, and travel contribute to the spread of infectious diseases and increase the risk of pandemics.

Economic Disruptions: Pandemics can lead to widespread economic disruptions, including supply chain disruptions, business closures, layoffs, and reduced consumer spending. These disruptions can have ripple effects across industries and financial markets, impacting investment portfolios and asset values.

Market Volatility: Pandemics often result in heightened market volatility as investors react to uncertainty and risk aversion. Stock markets may experience sharp declines, currency exchange rates may fluctuate, and commodity prices may be affected as investors adjust their portfolios in response to changing economic conditions.

Potential Impact of Pandemic Risk:

Pandemic risk can have several implications for investment portfolios, including:

Market Volatility: Pandemics can lead to increased market volatility as investors react to uncertainty and changing economic conditions. Stock markets may experience sharp fluctuations, and asset prices may be affected by changes in investor sentiment and risk appetite.

Economic Recession: Pandemics can trigger economic recessions as businesses face disruptions to operations, supply chains, and consumer demand. Economic contractions can lead to job losses, corporate bankruptcies, and declines in GDP growth, affecting investment returns and asset values.

Sectoral and Regional Impacts: Pandemics may disproportionately affect certain sectors and regions, depending on factors such as industry exposure, geographic location, and government response measures. Industries such as travel, hospitality, and retail may be particularly vulnerable to pandemic-related disruptions.

Strategies for Managing Pandemic Risk:

Effective management of pandemic risk involves implementing strategies to mitigate exposure and build resilience within investment portfolios. Strategies for managing pandemic risk include:

Diversification: Diversifying investment portfolios across asset classes, sectors, and regions to reduce exposure to pandemic-related risks and enhance portfolio resilience.

Scenario Analysis: Conducting scenario analysis to assess the potential impact of different pandemic scenarios on investment portfolios and identifying strategies to mitigate risk.

Contingency Planning: Developing and implementing contingency plans to respond to pandemic-related disruptions, including business continuity plans, supply chain diversification, and liquidity management strategies.

Stay Informed: Staying informed about developments related to infectious diseases, government response measures, and economic indicators to anticipate changes in market conditions and adjust investment strategies accordingly.

Conclusion:

Pandemic risk poses significant challenges for investors, with the potential to disrupt economies, industries, and financial markets. By understanding the nature of pandemic risk, its potential impact, and implementing effective risk management strategies, investors can mitigate the risk of pandemics and protect their investment portfolios from adverse effects. In the chapters to come, we will explore advanced techniques for managing pandemic risk and delve deeper into the intricacies of portfolio risk management.

Chapter: Beyond Traditional Risks: Navigating Additional Risks in Investment Portfolios

In addition to the well-known risks such as market, credit, liquidity, and operational risks, investors must navigate a diverse array of additional risks that can influence investment portfolios. Geopolitical risk, regulatory risk, environmental risk, cybersecurity risk, and pandemic risk are just a few examples of the additional risks that investors must consider in their risk management strategies. Understanding the nature of these risks and implementing appropriate risk management practices is crucial for investors to enhance their ability to navigate the complexities of the financial markets and achieve their investment objectives. In this chapter, we explore these additional risks and discuss strategies for effectively managing them within investment portfolios.

Geopolitical Risk:

Geopolitical risk refers to the potential for political instability, conflicts, or geopolitical events to impact investment markets and assets. Factors such as trade disputes, military conflicts, regulatory changes, and changes in government policies can all contribute to geopolitical risk. Investors may experience heightened market volatility, currency fluctuations, and uncertainty in regions or countries affected by geopolitical tensions.

Regulatory Risk:

Regulatory risk arises from changes in laws, regulations, or government policies that affect investment markets and assets. Regulatory changes can impact industries, businesses, and investment strategies, leading to compliance challenges, increased costs, or changes in market dynamics. Investors must stay informed about regulatory developments and adapt their investment strategies accordingly to mitigate regulatory risk.

Environmental Risk:

Environmental risk relates to the potential for environmental factors such as climate change, natural disasters, and environmental regulations to impact investment portfolios. Climate-related events such as hurricanes, wildfires, and floods can cause physical damage to assets and disrupt business operations, leading to financial losses. Additionally, regulatory efforts to address climate change and environmental sustainability can affect industries and businesses, influencing investment decisions and performance.

Cybersecurity Risk:

Cybersecurity risk refers to the potential for cyber-attacks, data breaches, and IT security incidents to impact investment portfolios and organizations. With the increasing reliance on technology and digital infrastructure, cybersecurity threats have become a significant concern for investors and businesses alike. Cyber-attacks can result in financial losses, reputational damage, regulatory fines, and legal liabilities, highlighting the importance of robust cybersecurity measures and risk management practices.

Pandemic Risk:

Pandemic risk pertains to the potential for widespread infectious diseases, such as the COVID-19 pandemic, to disrupt economies, industries, and financial markets. Pandemics can lead to supply chain disruptions, business closures, market volatility, and economic recession, impacting investment portfolios and asset values. Investors must consider the potential impact of pandemics on their investment strategies and incorporate contingency plans to mitigate pandemic risk.

Conclusion:

In addition to traditional risks, investors must navigate a variety of additional risks that can influence investment portfolios. Geopolitical risk, regulatory risk, environmental risk, cybersecurity risk, and pandemic risk are just a few examples of these additional risks. By understanding the nature of these risks and implementing appropriate risk management practices, investors can enhance their ability to navigate the complexities of the financial markets and achieve their investment objectives. In the chapters to come, we will explore advanced techniques for managing these and other types of risks and delve deeper into the intricacies of portfolio risk management.

Chapter: The Role of Risk Tolerance and Risk Appetite in Portfolio Construction

Risk tolerance and risk appetite are crucial concepts in portfolio construction, guiding investors in determining the level of risk they are willing and able to accept in pursuit of their investment objectives. Understanding these concepts is essential for constructing investment portfolios that align with investors' financial goals, time horizons, and risk preferences. In this chapter, we explore the definitions of risk tolerance and risk appetite, their significance in portfolio construction, and strategies for incorporating them into investment decision-making.

Defining Risk Tolerance and Risk Appetite:

Risk Tolerance: Risk tolerance refers to an investor's ability and willingness to withstand fluctuations in the value of their investment portfolio. It is influenced by factors such as investment time horizon, financial goals, income needs, and psychological disposition toward risk. Investors with a high-risk tolerance are willing to accept greater fluctuations in portfolio value in exchange for the potential for higher returns, while investors with a low risk tolerance prioritize capital preservation and are less willing to accept volatility.

Risk Appetite: Risk appetite, on the other hand, refers to an investor's willingness to take on risk in pursuit of investment returns. It reflects the investor's willingness to embrace uncertainty and volatility in the pursuit of potentially higher investment gains. Risk appetite is influenced by factors such as investment objectives, investment horizon, investment experience, and market outlook. Investors with a high-risk appetite are comfortable taking on greater levels of risk in their investment portfolios, while investors with a low-risk appetite prefer more conservative investment strategies with lower levels of risk.

Significance in Portfolio Construction:

Risk tolerance and risk appetite play a critical role in portfolio construction, helping investors determine the appropriate mix of assets and investment strategies to achieve their financial goals while managing risk effectively. Considerations for incorporating risk tolerance and risk appetite into portfolio construction include:

Asset Allocation: Asset allocation involves determining the mix of asset classes, such as stocks, bonds, cash, and alternative investments, within an investment portfolio. Risk tolerance and risk appetite inform asset allocation decisions by guiding investors in selecting asset classes that align with their risk preferences and investment objectives. For example, investors with a high-risk tolerance and risk appetite may allocate a larger portion of their portfolio to equities for the potential for higher returns, while investors with a low risk tolerance may prefer a more conservative allocation with a higher allocation to fixed-income securities.

Diversification: Diversification is a risk management strategy that involves spreading investment risk across different asset classes, sectors, and regions to reduce the impact of individual investment losses on the overall portfolio. Risk tolerance and risk appetite influence diversification decisions by guiding investors in determining the appropriate level of diversification based on their risk preferences and investment objectives. For example, investors with a higher risk tolerance and risk appetite may tolerate higher levels of concentration in individual securities or sectors, while investors with a lower risk tolerance may prefer a more diversified portfolio to reduce risk exposure.

Investment Strategy Selection: Investment strategies, such as passive investing, active investing, value investing, growth investing, and tactical asset allocation, differ in their risk-return profiles and investment approaches. Risk tolerance and risk appetite help investors select investment strategies that align with their risk preferences, investment objectives, and investment horizon. For example, investors with a high-risk tolerance and risk appetite may be more inclined to pursue aggressive investment strategies with a focus on growth and capital appreciation, while investors with a low risk tolerance may prefer more conservative investment strategies with a focus on capital preservation and income generation.

Strategies for Incorporating Risk Tolerance and Risk Appetite:

Risk Assessment: Conducting a comprehensive risk assessment to evaluate an investor's risk tolerance and risk appetite is the first step in incorporating these factors into portfolio construction. Risk assessment tools, risk tolerance questionnaires, and discussions with financial advisors can help investors determine their risk tolerance and risk appetite levels.

Goal Alignment: Aligning investment goals with risk tolerance and risk appetite is essential for constructing investment portfolios that meet investors' financial objectives while managing risk effectively. Investors should consider their investment goals, time horizon, income needs, and risk preferences when determining the appropriate level of risk for their portfolios.

Regular Review: Risk tolerance and risk appetite are not static and may change over time due to changes in financial circumstances, market conditions, and investment objectives. Regularly reviewing and reassessing risk tolerance and risk appetite allows investors to adjust their investment portfolios accordingly and ensure alignment with their evolving financial goals and risk preferences.

Conclusion:

Risk tolerance and risk appetite are fundamental concepts in portfolio construction, guiding investors in determining the appropriate level of risk for their investment portfolios. By understanding their risk tolerance and risk appetite levels and incorporating these factors into portfolio construction, investors can construct investment portfolios that align with their financial goals, time horizons, and risk preferences while effectively managing risk. In the chapters to come, we will explore advanced techniques for portfolio construction and delve deeper into the intricacies of risk management in investment portfolios.

Chapter: Historical Perspectives on Risk Management in Finance and Insurance Industries

The practice of risk management in finance and insurance industries has evolved significantly over time, shaped by historical events, regulatory changes, and advancements in financial theory and technology. Understanding the historical perspectives on risk management provides valuable insights into the development of risk management practices and their relevance in contemporary financial markets. In this chapter, we explore the historical evolution of risk management in finance and insurance industries, highlighting key milestones, challenges, and innovations that have shaped the discipline.

Early Beginnings:

The origins of risk management can be traced back to ancient civilizations, where merchants and traders sought to mitigate risks associated with trade, transportation, and maritime ventures. Early risk management practices focused on diversification, insurance arrangements, and contractual agreements to protect against losses from natural disasters, theft, and commercial failures.

Development of Insurance:

The concept of insurance emerged in ancient societies as a means of pooling risks and providing financial protection against unforeseen events. In ancient Greece and Rome, mutual aid societies and benevolent associations provided rudimentary forms of insurance coverage for merchants, sailors, and craftsmen. Over time, insurance evolved into a formalized industry with the establishment of insurance companies, underwriting standards, and actuarial methods for assessing risk and setting premiums.

Risk Management in Banking:

In the banking industry, risk management practices evolved alongside developments in financial markets, banking regulations, and banking operations. Early banking practices focused on credit risk management, with bankers relying on personal relationships, collateral, and reputation to assess creditworthiness and mitigate default risk. With the expansion of banking activities and the rise of complex financial instruments, banks developed more sophisticated risk management techniques, such as portfolio diversification, credit scoring models, and risk-based capital requirements.

Modern Risk Management:

The modern era of risk management in finance and insurance industries began in the late 20th century, marked by advancements in financial theory, computational capabilities, and regulatory oversight. The introduction of modern portfolio theory by Harry Markowitz in the 1950s laid the foundation for quantitative risk management techniques, such as mean-variance optimization and portfolio diversification. The development of option pricing models, such as the Black-Scholes model, revolutionized risk management in financial markets by providing insights into pricing and hedging options and derivatives.

Challenges and Innovations:

Throughout history, risk management has faced various challenges, including financial crises, regulatory changes, and technological disruptions. The globalization of financial markets, the proliferation of complex financial products, and the interconnectedness of financial institutions have posed new challenges for risk management practitioners. In response, risk management has evolved to incorporate new methodologies, such as value-at-risk (VaR), stress testing, and scenario analysis, to assess and manage risks in increasingly complex and dynamic markets.

Regulatory Framework:

The regulatory landscape has played a significant role in shaping risk management practices in finance and insurance industries. Regulatory initiatives, such as the Basel Accords for banking regulation and Solvency II for insurance regulation, have imposed requirements for capital adequacy, risk measurement, and risk governance to enhance the stability and resilience of financial institutions. Regulatory oversight has also focused on improving transparency, risk disclosure, and risk management practices to promote market integrity and investor protection.

Conclusion:

The historical perspectives on risk management in finance and insurance industries highlight the evolution of risk management practices over time, from ancient civilizations to the modern era of global financial markets. By understanding the historical context, challenges, and innovations that have shaped risk management, practitioners can gain valuable insights into effective risk management strategies and approaches in contemporary financial markets. In the chapters to come, we will explore advanced topics in risk management and delve deeper into the application of risk management principles in finance and insurance industries.

Chapter: Principles of Portfolio Management: Overview of Portfolio Theory and Diversification

Portfolio management is a fundamental practice in finance that involves the selection, allocation, and management of investments to achieve investment objectives while managing risk effectively. Central to portfolio management is portfolio theory, which provides the framework for understanding the benefits of diversification and the trade-offs between risk and return. In this chapter, we provide an overview of portfolio theory and the principles of diversification, exploring how these concepts inform portfolio management strategies and decision-making.

Portfolio Theory:

Portfolio theory, pioneered by Harry Markowitz in the 1950s, revolutionized the field of finance by introducing the concept of diversification and the principles of risk-return trade-offs. At its core, portfolio theory asserts that investors can achieve higher returns for a given level of risk, or reduce risk for a given level of return, by diversifying their investment portfolios across multiple assets. The key insights of portfolio theory include:

Diversification: Diversification is the principle of spreading investment risk across a range of assets with different risk-return profiles. By combining assets with low or negative correlations, investors can reduce the overall volatility of their portfolios and enhance risk-adjusted returns. Diversification allows investors to mitigate the impact of individual asset losses on the overall portfolio and smooth out investment returns over time.

Risk-Return Trade-off: Portfolio theory posits that there is a trade-off between risk and return, where higher returns are generally associated with higher levels of risk. Investors must balance their desire for higher returns with their willingness to accept greater levels of risk. The efficient frontier represents the set of portfolios that offer the highest expected returns for a given level of risk, allowing investors to identify optimal portfolios based on their risk preferences.

Asset Allocation: Asset allocation is the process of determining the mix of asset classes, such as stocks, bonds, cash, and alternative investments, within an investment portfolio. Asset allocation decisions are guided by investors' investment objectives, risk tolerance, time horizon, and market outlook. Strategic asset allocation involves setting long-term target allocations based on expected returns and risk characteristics of different asset classes, while tactical asset allocation involves making short-term adjustments to exploit market opportunities or manage risk.

Diversification:

Diversification is a core principle of portfolio management that aims to reduce investment risk by spreading exposure across different asset classes, sectors, and regions. The benefits of diversification include:

Risk Reduction: Diversification allows investors to reduce the overall volatility of their portfolios by spreading investment risk across multiple assets with different risk-return profiles. By combining assets with low correlations, investors can mitigate the impact of individual asset losses on the overall portfolio.

Enhanced Risk-Adjusted Returns: Diversification can improve risk-adjusted returns by reducing portfolio volatility while maintaining or increasing expected returns. By diversifying across assets with different return drivers, investors can capture the benefits of asset class diversification and improve portfolio efficiency.

Smoother Investment Returns: Diversification can smooth out investment returns over time by reducing the impact of market fluctuations and individual asset volatility. A well-diversified portfolio is less susceptible to extreme fluctuations and can provide more stable long-term returns.

Practical Considerations:

In practice, implementing diversification requires careful consideration of factors such as asset class selection, correlation analysis, portfolio rebalancing, and risk management. Investors should assess their risk tolerance, investment objectives, and time horizon to determine the appropriate level of diversification for their portfolios. Additionally, monitoring portfolio performance and periodically rebalancing the portfolio to maintain target asset allocations is essential for effective diversification.

Conclusion:

Portfolio management principles, rooted in portfolio theory and diversification, provide the foundation for constructing and managing investment portfolios. By understanding the benefits of diversification and the principles of risk-return trade-offs, investors can construct well-diversified portfolios that align with their investment objectives and risk preferences. In the chapters to come, we will explore advanced topics in portfolio management and delve deeper into portfolio construction, asset allocation, and risk management strategies.

Chapter: Asset Allocation Strategies for Managing Risk and Return

Asset allocation is a crucial component of portfolio management, influencing both risk and return characteristics of investment portfolios. By strategically allocating investments across different asset classes, investors can effectively manage risk and enhance portfolio returns. In this chapter, we explore various asset allocation strategies and their implications for managing risk and return in investment portfolios.

Strategic Asset Allocation:

Strategic asset allocation involves setting long-term target allocations to different asset classes based on investors' investment objectives, risk tolerance, and time horizon. The goal of strategic asset allocation is to create a well-diversified portfolio that balances risk and return characteristics to achieve investors' financial goals over the long term. Key considerations for strategic asset allocation include:

Risk-Return Profiles: Different asset classes, such as stocks, bonds, cash, and alternative investments, have distinct risk-return profiles. Stocks, for example, historically offer higher returns but also come with higher volatility, while bonds provide income and stability but typically offer lower returns. Strategic asset allocation aims to optimize the mix of asset classes to achieve desired risk and return objectives.

Diversification Benefits: Strategic asset allocation leverages the benefits of diversification by spreading investment risk across multiple asset classes with low or negative correlations. By combining assets with different return drivers and risk characteristics, investors can reduce portfolio volatility and enhance risk-adjusted returns.

Long-Term Perspective: Strategic asset allocation takes a long-term perspective, focusing on the fundamental drivers of asset class returns, such as economic growth, interest rates, and inflation. Investors set target allocations based on their long-term investment horizon and periodically rebalance the portfolio to maintain desired asset class weights.

Tactical Asset Allocation:

Tactical asset allocation involves making short-term adjustments to portfolio allocations based on market conditions, economic outlook, and investment opportunities. Unlike strategic asset allocation, which follows a predefined target allocation, tactical asset allocation allows investors to exploit market inefficiencies or manage short-term risks. Key considerations for tactical asset allocation include:

Market Valuations: Tactical asset allocation considers market valuations and asset price trends to identify opportunities for adjusting portfolio allocations. For example, if certain asset classes become overvalued or undervalued relative to their historical averages, investors may adjust allocations to capitalize on potential market mispricing.

Economic Indicators: Tactical asset allocation takes into account macroeconomic indicators, such as GDP growth, inflation rates, interest rates, and unemployment levels, to assess the overall economic environment and its implications for asset class performance. Changes in economic conditions may warrant adjustments to portfolio allocations to align with changing market dynamics.

Active Management: Tactical asset allocation requires active management and ongoing monitoring of market conditions and investment opportunities. Investors must have the flexibility to adjust portfolio allocations in response to changing market conditions and incorporate new information into their investment decision-making process.

Combining Strategies:

Many investors utilize a combination of strategic and tactical asset allocation strategies to achieve their investment objectives while managing risk effectively. This approach, known as dynamic asset allocation, allows investors to benefit from the stability and long-term focus of strategic asset allocation while also taking advantage of short-term opportunities identified through tactical adjustments.

Conclusion:

Asset allocation plays a crucial role in managing risk and return in investment portfolios. By strategically allocating investments across different asset classes, investors can achieve diversification benefits, optimize risk-return profiles, and enhance long-term portfolio performance. Whether through strategic asset allocation, tactical asset allocation, or a combination of both, investors can tailor their asset allocation strategies to align with their investment objectives, risk tolerance, and market outlook. In the chapters to come, we will explore advanced techniques for asset allocation and delve deeper into the intricacies of portfolio management.

Chapter: Modern Portfolio Management Techniques: Mean-Variance Analysis and the Capital Asset Pricing Model (CAPM)

Modern portfolio management techniques provide investors with sophisticated tools for optimizing investment portfolios, balancing risk, and return, and achieving diversification benefits. Two prominent techniques in modern portfolio management are mean-variance analysis and the Capital Asset Pricing Model (CAPM). In this chapter, we explore these techniques, their underlying principles, and their application in portfolio construction and risk management.

Mean-Variance Analysis:

Mean-variance analysis, developed by Harry Markowitz in the 1950s, is a cornerstone of modern portfolio theory. It provides a framework for quantifying risk and return characteristics of investment portfolios and identifying optimal portfolios that offer the highest expected return for a given level of risk. Key concepts of mean-variance analysis include:

Expected Return: Mean-variance analysis starts by estimating the expected returns of individual assets based on historical data, fundamental analysis, or market forecasts. Expected return represents the average return an investor can expect to earn from holding an asset over a specified time horizon.

Risk Measurement: Mean-variance analysis quantifies risk as the variance or standard deviation of asset returns, representing the volatility or dispersion of returns around the expected return. Standard deviation measures the degree of uncertainty or variability in investment returns and serves as a proxy for investment risk.

Efficient Frontier: The efficient frontier is the set of portfolios that offer the highest expected return for a given level of risk or the lowest risk for a given level of return. Mean-variance analysis seeks to identify optimal portfolios along the efficient frontier that provide the best risk-return trade-offs based on investors' risk preferences.

Portfolio Diversification: Mean-variance analysis highlights the benefits of portfolio diversification in reducing investment risk. By combining assets with low or negative correlations, investors can achieve diversification benefits and reduce portfolio volatility without sacrificing expected returns.

Capital Asset Pricing Model (CAPM):

The Capital Asset Pricing Model (CAPM), developed by William Sharpe, John Lintner, and Jack Treynor in the 1960s, is another key tool in modern portfolio management. CAPM provides a framework for estimating expected returns and assessing the risk-adjusted performance of investment portfolios. Key concepts of CAPM include:

Systematic Risk and Beta: CAPM distinguishes between systematic risk, which represents the risk that cannot be diversified away, and unsystematic risk, which can be eliminated through diversification. Beta is a measure of an asset's systematic risk, representing its sensitivity to movements in the overall market.

Security Market Line (SML): The Security Market Line (SML) is a graphical representation of the CAPM, depicting the relationship between expected return and systematic risk for individual assets or portfolios. Assets that lie above the SML are considered undervalued, while assets that lie below the SML are considered overvalued.

Risk-Free Rate and Market Risk Premium: CAPM incorporates the risk-free rate, representing the return on a risk-free investment such as Treasury bills, and the market risk premium, representing the additional return investors require for bearing systematic risk. The market risk premium is calculated as the difference between the expected return on the market portfolio and the risk-free rate.

Application in Portfolio Management:

Mean-variance analysis and CAPM are widely used in portfolio management for asset allocation, risk assessment, and performance evaluation. Portfolio managers use mean-variance optimization techniques to construct efficient portfolios along the efficient frontier, balancing risk and return objectives based on investors' risk preferences. CAPM provides a framework for estimating expected returns and assessing the performance of investment portfolios relative to their systematic risk exposure.

Limitations and Considerations:

While mean-variance analysis and CAPM are valuable tools in portfolio management, they have certain limitations and assumptions that may affect their applicability in real-world investment scenarios. Assumptions such as normality of returns, static correlations, and rational investor behavior may not always hold true in practice. Additionally, CAPM relies on market efficiency assumptions and may not fully capture the complexities of asset pricing in real-world markets.

Conclusion:

Mean-variance analysis and CAPM are powerful tools in modern portfolio management, providing investors with frameworks for optimizing investment portfolios and assessing risk-adjusted performance. By leveraging these techniques, investors can construct well-diversified portfolios that balance risk and return objectives and achieve their investment goals over the long term. However, it is essential for investors to recognize the limitations and assumptions of these models and supplement them with additional analysis and judgment in real-world investment decision-making. In the chapters to come, we will explore advanced techniques for portfolio management and delve deeper into the intricacies of risk management and asset allocation strategies.

Chapter: Incorporating Alternative Investments and Derivatives into Portfolios

In today's dynamic and complex financial markets, investors seek to enhance portfolio diversification, manage risk, and potentially boost returns by incorporating alternative investments and derivatives into their portfolios. Alternative investments, such as hedge funds, private equity, real estate, and commodities, offer unique risk-return characteristics and low correlation with traditional asset classes. Derivatives, such as options, futures, and swaps, provide investors with tools for hedging, speculation, and portfolio management. In this chapter, we explore the considerations and strategies for incorporating alternative investments and derivatives into portfolios.

Diversification Benefits of Alternative Investments:

Alternative investments offer diversification benefits by providing exposure to asset classes with low correlation to traditional stocks and bonds. By adding alternative investments to a portfolio, investors can reduce overall portfolio volatility and enhance risk-adjusted returns. Different types of alternative investments offer varying risk-return profiles and may serve different objectives in portfolio construction:

Hedge Funds: Hedge funds employ various strategies, including long-short equity, event-driven, macro, and relative value, to generate returns independent of traditional market indices. Hedge funds often have lower correlations with equity and bond markets, making them attractive diversification tools for institutional and high-net-worth investors.

Private Equity: Private equity investments involve investing in privately held companies or assets with the goal of generating long-term capital appreciation. Private equity offers exposure to a different set of investment opportunities than public equity markets and may provide higher returns and lower volatility over the long term.

Real Estate: Real estate investments include direct ownership of properties, real estate investment trusts (REITs), and real estate funds. Real estate offers diversification benefits due to its low correlation with traditional asset classes and potential for income generation and capital appreciation.

Commodities: Commodities, such as gold, oil, and agricultural products, provide exposure to physical assets with unique supply-demand dynamics. Commodities can serve as inflation hedges and diversification tools in investment portfolios, particularly during periods of economic uncertainty or inflationary pressures.

Strategies for Incorporating Derivatives:

Derivatives are financial instruments whose value is derived from an underlying asset, index, or benchmark. Derivatives offer investors opportunities for risk management, speculation, and portfolio management. Common types of derivatives include options, futures, forwards, and swaps. Strategies for incorporating derivatives into portfolios include:

Hedging: Derivatives can be used to hedge against specific risks in investment portfolios, such as market risk, interest rate risk, currency risk, and commodity price risk. For example, investors can use options or futures contracts to hedge against adverse movements in stock prices or interest rates.

Speculation: Derivatives allow investors to take directional views on the future movements of underlying assets or indices. Speculative strategies using derivatives include buying call options to profit from rising stock prices or selling futures contracts to profit from falling commodity prices.

Portfolio Management: Derivatives can be used as portfolio management tools to adjust portfolio exposures, enhance returns, or manage risk. For example, investors can use index futures or exchange-traded funds (ETFs) to adjust asset allocations quickly and efficiently.

Considerations and Risks:

While alternative investments and derivatives offer potential benefits, they also come with unique considerations and risks that investors must carefully evaluate:

Complexity: Alternative investments and derivatives can be complex and may require specialized knowledge and expertise to understand and evaluate effectively. Investors should conduct thorough due diligence and seek advice from qualified professionals before investing in alternative assets or derivatives.

Liquidity: Some alternative investments, such as private equity and real estate, may have limited liquidity and longer investment horizons. Investors should consider the liquidity requirements of their investment portfolios and the potential impact of illiquidity on portfolio performance.

Counterparty Risk: Derivatives transactions involve counterparty risk, the risk that the counterparty to a derivative contract may default on its obligations. Investors should assess the creditworthiness and financial stability of counterparties when entering into derivative transactions.

Regulatory and Legal Risks: Alternative investments and derivatives are subject to regulatory oversight and legal risks, including compliance with regulatory requirements, tax implications, and potential legal disputes. Investors should understand the regulatory and legal framework governing alternative investments and derivatives in their respective jurisdictions.

Conclusion:

Incorporating alternative investments and derivatives into portfolios can enhance diversification, manage risk, and potentially improve returns for investors. Alternative investments offer exposure to non-traditional asset classes with low correlation to stocks and bonds, while derivatives provide tools for hedging, speculation, and portfolio management. However, investors should carefully evaluate the unique considerations and risks associated with alternative investments and derivatives and ensure that they align with their investment objectives, risk tolerance, and overall portfolio strategy. In the chapters to come, we will explore advanced techniques for portfolio construction and risk management, including the integration of alternative investments and derivatives into investment portfolios.

Chapter: Risk Assessment and Measurement: Quantitative Methods for Measuring and Assessing Portfolio Risk

Risk assessment and measurement are critical components of portfolio management, enabling investors to quantify and understand the potential risks associated with their investment portfolios. In today's complex financial markets, investors employ quantitative methods to measure and assess portfolio risk, allowing them to make informed decisions about asset allocation, risk management, and portfolio construction. In this chapter, we explore various quantitative methods for measuring and assessing portfolio risk.

Standard Deviation:

Standard deviation is a widely used measure of portfolio risk that quantifies the dispersion of returns around the portfolio's average return. A higher standard deviation indicates greater volatility and uncertainty in portfolio returns, while a lower standard deviation suggests more stable and predictable returns. Standard deviation is calculated as the square root of the variance of portfolio returns and provides a simple yet effective measure of portfolio risk.

Value-at-Risk (VaR):

Value-at-Risk (VaR) is a statistical measure of downside risk that estimates the maximum potential loss a portfolio may incur over a specified time horizon at a given confidence level. VaR provides investors with a single number that represents the worst-case loss the portfolio is expected to experience within a certain probability level. VaR can be calculated using various statistical methods, including historical simulation, parametric methods, and Monte Carlo simulation. VaR allows investors to assess the potential downside risk of their portfolios and set risk limits based on their risk tolerance and investment objectives.

Conditional Value-at-Risk (CVaR):

Conditional Value-at-Risk (CVaR), also known as expected shortfall, is a risk measure that quantifies the expected loss in the tail of the distribution beyond the VaR threshold. Unlike VaR, which focuses on the maximum loss within a specified confidence level, CVaR considers the average loss in the worst-case scenarios that exceed the VaR threshold. CVaR provides a more comprehensive measure of downside risk and is often used in conjunction with VaR to provide a more complete picture of portfolio risk.

Sharpe Ratio:

The Sharpe Ratio is a risk-adjusted measure of portfolio performance that compares the excess return of a portfolio to its volatility, as measured by standard deviation. The Sharpe Ratio indicates how much excess return an investor receives for each unit of risk taken. A higher Sharpe Ratio suggests better risk-adjusted performance, while a lower Sharpe Ratio indicates lower risk-adjusted performance. The Sharpe Ratio helps investors evaluate the risk-adjusted return of their portfolios and compare the performance of different investment strategies.

Beta:

Beta is a measure of systematic risk that quantifies the sensitivity of a portfolio's returns to changes in the overall market, as represented by a benchmark index such as the S&P 500. A beta greater than 1 indicates that the portfolio is more volatile than the market, while a beta less than 1 suggests that the portfolio is less volatile than the market. Beta helps investors understand the systematic risk exposure of their portfolios and assess how changes in market conditions may impact portfolio returns.

Conclusion:

Quantitative methods for measuring and assessing portfolio risk play a crucial role in portfolio management, allowing investors to quantify and understand the potential risks associated with their investment portfolios. Standard deviation, Value-at-Risk (VaR), Conditional Value-at-Risk (CVaR), Sharpe Ratio, and Beta are among the commonly used quantitative measures of portfolio risk that provide valuable insights into portfolio risk characteristics, performance, and exposure to market fluctuations. By employing quantitative risk assessment techniques, investors can make informed decisions about asset allocation, risk management, and portfolio construction, ultimately enhancing their ability to achieve their investment objectives while managing risk effectively. In the chapters to come, we will explore advanced techniques for portfolio risk management and delve deeper into the intricacies of risk assessment and measurement.

Chapter: Value at Risk (VaR) and Other Risk Metrics

In portfolio management, accurately assessing and quantifying risk is essential for making informed investment decisions and managing portfolio exposures effectively. Value at Risk (VaR) is one of the most widely used risk metrics that provides a measure of the potential loss a portfolio may incur over a specified time horizon at a given confidence level. However, VaR is just one of many risk metrics used by investors to evaluate and manage portfolio risk. In this chapter, we explore Value at Risk (VaR) and other important risk metrics employed in portfolio management.

Value at Risk (VaR):

Value at Risk (VaR) is a statistical measure of downside risk that estimates the maximum potential loss a portfolio may experience over a specified time horizon at a given confidence level. VaR provides investors with a single number that represents the worst-case loss the portfolio is expected to incur within a certain probability level. VaR can be calculated using various statistical methods, including historical simulation, parametric methods, and Monte Carlo simulation. Despite its widespread use, VaR has limitations and assumptions that investors should consider, including the assumption of normality in return distributions and the reliance on historical data.

Conditional Value at Risk (CVaR):

Conditional Value at Risk (CVaR), also known as expected shortfall, is a risk measure that quantifies the expected loss in the tail of the distribution beyond the VaR threshold. Unlike VaR, which focuses on the maximum loss within a specified confidence level, CVaR considers the average loss in the worst-case scenarios that exceed the VaR threshold. CVaR provides a more comprehensive measure of downside risk and is often used in conjunction with VaR to provide a more complete picture of portfolio risk.

Sharpe Ratio:

The Sharpe Ratio is a risk-adjusted measure of portfolio performance that compares the excess return of a portfolio to its volatility, as measured by standard deviation. The Sharpe Ratio indicates how much excess return an investor receives for each unit of risk taken. A higher Sharpe Ratio suggests better risk-adjusted performance, while a lower Sharpe Ratio indicates lower risk-adjusted performance. The Sharpe Ratio helps investors evaluate the risk-adjusted return of their portfolios and compare the performance of different investment strategies.

Beta:

Beta is a measure of systematic risk that quantifies the sensitivity of a portfolio's returns to changes in the overall market, as represented by a benchmark index such as the S&P 500. A beta greater than 1 indicates that the portfolio is more volatile than the market, while a beta less than 1 suggests that the portfolio is less volatile than the market. Beta helps investors understand the systematic risk exposure of their portfolios and assess how changes in market conditions may impact portfolio returns.

Tracking Error:

Tracking error measures, the deviation of a portfolio's returns from its benchmark index, representing the active risk associated with portfolio management decisions. Tracking error provides insights into the effectiveness of portfolio management in generating excess returns relative to the benchmark. A higher tracking error indicates greater deviation from the benchmark and potentially higher active risk.

Conclusion:

Value at Risk (VaR) and other risk metrics play a crucial role in portfolio management, providing investors with tools to quantify, assess, and manage portfolio risk effectively. While VaR is a widely used measure of downside risk, investors should complement it with other risk metrics such as Conditional Value at Risk (CVaR), Sharpe Ratio, Beta, and Tracking Error to gain a comprehensive understanding of portfolio risk characteristics, performance, and exposure to market fluctuations. By employing a combination of risk metrics, investors can make informed investment decisions, construct well-diversified portfolios, and achieve their investment objectives while managing risk effectively. In the chapters to come, we will explore advanced techniques for portfolio risk management and delve deeper into the intricacies of risk assessment and measurement.

Chapter: Stress Testing and Scenario Analysis for Evaluating Portfolio Resilience

In the face of unpredictable market conditions and economic uncertainties, assessing the resilience of investment portfolios is paramount for investors and portfolio managers. Stress testing and scenario analysis are essential techniques used in portfolio management to evaluate how portfolios may perform under adverse conditions and identify potential vulnerabilities. In this chapter, we explore stress testing and scenario analysis as powerful tools for assessing portfolio resilience and enhancing risk management.

Stress Testing:

Stress testing involves subjecting investment portfolios to extreme, yet plausible, market scenarios to assess their resilience and potential vulnerabilities. Unlike traditional risk metrics that focus on historical data and assumptions of normal market conditions, stress testing evaluates portfolio performance under severe market shocks and tail events. Key steps in stress testing include:

Scenario Generation: Stress tests involve creating hypothetical scenarios that represent extreme market conditions or adverse events, such as financial crises, market crashes, or geopolitical upheavals. Scenarios are designed to capture the most significant sources of risk and uncertainty relevant to the portfolio's investment universe.

Impact Analysis: Once scenarios are defined, the impact of each scenario on portfolio returns, volatility, and other risk metrics is analyzed using quantitative models and simulations. Stress testing helps identify potential losses, liquidity constraints, and risk concentrations within the portfolio under adverse market conditions.

Risk Mitigation Strategies: Based on the results of stress testing, investors can develop risk mitigation strategies and contingency plans to address identified vulnerabilities and enhance portfolio resilience. These strategies may include adjusting asset allocations, hedging exposures, diversifying investments, or implementing risk management measures.

Scenario Analysis:

Scenario analysis involves evaluating the potential impact of specific macroeconomic or market scenarios on investment portfolios. Unlike stress testing, which focuses on extreme and adverse scenarios, scenario analysis examines a range of possible outcomes and their probabilities of occurrence. Scenario analysis helps investors understand how different market scenarios may affect portfolio performance and inform investment decisions. Key aspects of scenario analysis include:

Scenario Selection: Scenario analysis involves selecting a range of plausible scenarios that reflect different economic, financial, and geopolitical conditions. Scenarios may include baseline, upside, and downside scenarios, as well as specific events or developments relevant to the portfolio's investment strategy.

Sensitivity Analysis: Once scenarios are defined, sensitivity analysis is conducted to assess the sensitivity of portfolio returns and risk metrics to changes in key assumptions or inputs. Sensitivity analysis helps identify the most significant drivers of portfolio performance and potential areas of risk concentration.

Decision-Making: Scenario analysis provides valuable insights into the potential outcomes and risks associated with different market scenarios, allowing investors to make informed investment decisions and adjust portfolio strategies accordingly. Scenario analysis helps investors prepare for a range of possible future scenarios and adapt their investment approach to changing market conditions.

Conclusion:

Stress testing and scenario analysis are essential techniques for evaluating portfolio resilience and enhancing risk management in investment portfolios. By subjecting portfolios to extreme market scenarios and assessing their performance under adverse conditions, investors can identify potential vulnerabilities, develop risk mitigation strategies, and enhance portfolio resilience. Stress testing and scenario analysis provide valuable insights into the potential impact of market shocks, economic downturns, and geopolitical events on investment portfolios, helping investors make informed decisions and navigate uncertain market environments effectively. In the chapters to come, we will explore advanced techniques for portfolio risk management and delve deeper into the intricacies of stress testing, scenario analysis, and risk mitigation strategies.

Chapter: The Importance of Robust Risk Modeling and Data Analytics

In today's complex and interconnected financial markets, robust risk modeling and data analytics are essential for effective portfolio management and risk mitigation. As investment portfolios grow increasingly diverse and sophisticated, investors rely on advanced quantitative techniques and data-driven insights to quantify, assess, and manage portfolio risk effectively. In this chapter, we explore the importance of robust risk modeling and data analytics in enhancing risk management practices and improving investment decision-making processes.

Quantitative Risk Modeling:

Quantitative risk modeling involves using mathematical and statistical techniques to quantify and analyze portfolio risk. By incorporating historical data, probability theory, and advanced modeling methodologies, quantitative risk models help investors understand the potential sources of risk within their portfolios and assess the likelihood and impact of adverse events. Key aspects of quantitative risk modeling include:

Risk Identification: Quantitative risk models enable investors to identify and quantify various types of risk within their portfolios, including market risk, credit risk, liquidity risk, and operational risk. By categorizing and quantifying different sources of risk, investors can develop a comprehensive understanding of portfolio risk exposures.

Risk Measurement: Quantitative risk models provide metrics for measuring and quantifying portfolio risk, such as Value at Risk (VaR), Conditional Value at Risk (CVaR), Sharpe Ratio, and Tracking Error. These risk metrics help investors assess the potential downside risk, risk-adjusted performance, and active risk associated with their portfolios.

Risk Attribution: Quantitative risk models allow investors to attribute portfolio risk to specific assets, sectors, or factors, providing insights into the drivers of portfolio risk and performance. Risk attribution analysis helps investors identify risk concentrations, assess diversification benefits, and optimize portfolio allocations.

Data Analytics:

Data analytics involves collecting, processing, and analyzing large volumes of data to extract meaningful insights and inform decision-making processes. In portfolio management, data analytics plays a crucial role in identifying patterns, trends, and correlations in market data, economic indicators, and portfolio performance metrics. Key aspects of data analytics in portfolio management include:

Data Collection and Integration: Data analytics require access to a diverse range of data sources, including market data, economic indicators, financial statements, and alternative data sources. Integrating and consolidating data from multiple sources enables investors to gain a holistic view of market dynamics and portfolio performance.

Quantitative Analysis: Data analytics techniques, such as regression analysis, time-series analysis, and machine learning algorithms, enable investors to conduct quantitative analysis of market data and portfolio performance. By applying statistical methods and modeling techniques to historical data, investors can identify patterns, relationships, and anomalies in market behavior.

Predictive Modeling: Data analytics facilitate the development of predictive models that forecast future market trends, asset prices, and portfolio performance. Predictive modeling techniques, such as regression models, neural networks, and ensemble methods, help investors anticipate market movements, assess potential investment opportunities, and manage portfolio risk proactively.

Benefits of Robust Risk Modeling and Data Analytics:

Robust risk modeling and data analytics offer several benefits for portfolio management and risk mitigation, including:

Enhanced Risk Management: Robust risk modeling and data analytics enable investors to identify, quantify, and manage portfolio risk effectively, leading to improved risk-adjusted returns and reduced downside risk.

Informed Decision-Making: By leveraging quantitative techniques and data-driven insights, investors can make informed investment decisions, optimize portfolio allocations, and capitalize on market opportunities.

Adaptive Portfolio Strategies: Risk modeling and data analytics allow investors to adapt their portfolio strategies dynamically in response to changing market conditions, economic trends, and risk factors.

Performance Evaluation: Quantitative risk models and data analytics provide metrics for evaluating portfolio performance, tracking performance against benchmarks, and assessing the effectiveness of investment strategies.

Conclusion:

Robust risk modeling and data analytics are indispensable tools for portfolio management and risk mitigation in today's dynamic and complex financial markets. By leveraging quantitative techniques, statistical methods, and advanced modeling methodologies, investors can quantify, assess, and manage portfolio risk effectively, leading to improved investment outcomes and enhanced risk-adjusted returns. Furthermore, data analytics provide valuable insights into market dynamics, portfolio performance, and investment opportunities, enabling investors to make informed decisions and adapt their portfolio strategies to changing market conditions. In the chapters to come, we will explore advanced techniques for risk modeling, data analytics, and portfolio optimization, further enhancing our understanding of portfolio management practices in the modern financial landscape.

Chapter: Risk Management in the Insurance Industry: Understanding the Unique Risks Faced by Insurance Companies

Risk management is fundamental to the operations of insurance companies, which specialize in providing financial protection against various risks faced by individuals, businesses, and organizations. Unlike other financial institutions, insurance companies operate in a distinct risk landscape characterized by unique challenges and exposures. In this chapter, we delve into the intricacies of risk management in the insurance industry, exploring the distinctive risks faced by insurance companies and the strategies employed to mitigate these risks effectively.

Underwriting Risk:

Underwriting risk is inherent in the insurance business and arises from the uncertainty associated with estimating and pricing insurance policies. Insurance companies face the challenge of accurately assessing the likelihood and severity of future claims while setting premiums that are sufficient to cover expected losses and expenses. Underwriting risk encompasses factors such as adverse selection, moral hazard, and exposure to catastrophic events, which can impact the profitability and solvency of insurance companies.

Investment Risk:

Investment risk arises from the allocation of insurance company assets into various investment instruments, such as bonds, equities, real estate, and alternative investments. Insurance companies invest premiums collected from policyholders to generate investment income and meet future claim obligations. However, investment risk stems from market volatility, credit risk, interest rate fluctuations, and liquidity constraints, which can affect the value and performance of investment portfolios and impair the financial stability of insurance companies.

Reserving Risk:

Reserving risk refers to the uncertainty associated with estimating the reserves needed to cover future claim payments and policyholder obligations. Insurance companies must maintain adequate reserves to ensure that they can fulfill their obligations to policyholders and meet regulatory requirements. Reserving risk arises from factors such as adverse claims development, changes in loss patterns, and fluctuations in economic conditions, which can lead to reserve deficiencies and financial losses for insurance companies.

Operational Risk:

Operational risk encompasses a wide range of risks arising from internal processes, systems, and human factors within insurance companies. Operational risk includes risks related to underwriting, claims processing, policy administration, IT systems, fraud, compliance, and reputation. Insurance companies must implement robust internal controls, governance structures, and risk management practices to mitigate operational risk and safeguard the integrity and reliability of their operations.

Reinsurance and Catastrophe Risk:

Reinsurance plays a crucial role in mitigating insurance company risk by transferring a portion of risk exposure to other insurers or reinsurers. Reinsurance protects insurance companies against large or catastrophic losses that exceed their risk tolerance or capital capacity. Catastrophe risk refers to the potential for significant losses arising from natural disasters, such as hurricanes, earthquakes, floods, and wildfires, which can threaten the financial viability of insurance companies and necessitate the use of reinsurance and risk modeling techniques.

Regulatory and Compliance Risk:

Regulatory and compliance risk arises from the complex regulatory environment in which insurance companies operate, encompassing laws, regulations, and supervisory requirements imposed by regulatory authorities. Insurance companies must comply with various regulatory standards related to solvency, capital adequacy, financial reporting, consumer protection, and market conduct. Regulatory non-compliance can result in fines, penalties, reputational damage, and legal liabilities for insurance companies, highlighting the importance of effective regulatory risk management.

Conclusion:

Risk management is a cornerstone of the insurance industry, essential for protecting policyholders, preserving capital, and ensuring the long-term viability of insurance companies. Understanding the unique risks faced by insurance companies, including underwriting risk, investment risk, reserving risk, operational risk, reinsurance and catastrophe risk, and regulatory and compliance risk, is crucial for developing robust risk management strategies and maintaining financial resilience. By implementing effective risk management practices, insurance companies can mitigate risks, optimize performance, and fulfill their mission of providing financial security and protection to individuals and businesses against unforeseen events. In the chapters to come, we will explore advanced techniques and innovations in risk management, further enhancing our understanding of risk management practices in the insurance industry.

Chapter: Actuarial Principles and Methodologies for Risk Assessment

Actuarial science plays a pivotal role in the insurance industry by providing quantitative techniques and methodologies for assessing, pricing, and managing risks associated with insurance products. Actuaries utilize mathematical models, statistical analysis, and financial theory to evaluate the probability and impact of future events and determine appropriate premiums, reserves, and capital requirements. In this chapter, we delve into the fundamental principles and methodologies of actuarial science for risk assessment in the insurance industry.

Risk Identification and Classification:

The first step in actuarial risk assessment is identifying and classifying the various types of risks faced by insurance companies. Actuaries analyze historical data, industry trends, and policy characteristics to identify the sources of risk, including underwriting risk, investment risk, mortality risk, morbidity risk, longevity risk, and catastrophe risk. By categorizing risks based on their nature, origin, and impact, actuaries can develop appropriate risk management strategies and pricing models for insurance products.

Probability Theory and Statistical Analysis:

Probability theory and statistical analysis form the foundation of actuarial science, enabling actuaries to quantify the likelihood and severity of future events and estimate their impact on insurance portfolios. Actuaries use probability distributions, regression analysis, time-series models, and stochastic simulations to model the uncertainty and variability inherent in insurance risk. By analyzing historical data and projecting future trends, actuaries can assess the frequency and severity of claims, evaluate loss distributions, and calculate risk measures such as Value at Risk (VaR) and Conditional Value at Risk (CVaR).

Survival Analysis and Life Contingencies:

Survival analysis and life contingencies are essential techniques used in actuarial science for assessing mortality and morbidity risk in life insurance and annuity products. Actuaries analyze mortality tables, medical data, and demographic factors to estimate the probability of death or survival at different ages and durations. Survival models, such as the Kaplan-Meier estimator and Cox proportional hazards model, are used to analyze survival data and predict life expectancies, mortality rates, and survival probabilities. Life contingencies methods, such as life tables, life insurance reserves, and annuity valuations, are used to calculate premiums, reserves, and benefits for life insurance and annuity contracts.

Risk Modeling and Simulation:

Risk modeling and simulation techniques are employed by actuaries to model the stochastic nature of insurance risk and assess the impact of random events on insurance portfolios. Actuaries use simulation methods, such as Monte Carlo simulation and scenario analysis, to generate multiple scenarios of future outcomes based on probabilistic assumptions and input parameters. By simulating thousands of possible scenarios, actuaries can evaluate the distribution of potential outcomes, estimate risk measures, and quantify the uncertainty associated with insurance risk.

Financial Mathematics and Capital Management:

Financial mathematics and capital management are integral components of actuarial science, focusing on the valuation of insurance liabilities, determination of capital requirements, and optimization of capital allocation. Actuaries apply principles of present value, discounting, and interest theory to value future cash flows associated with insurance liabilities, including claim payments, reserves, and policyholder benefits. Capital management techniques, such as risk-based capital (RBC) models, economic capital models, and solvency regulations, are used to assess the financial strength and solvency of insurance companies and ensure adequate capitalization to withstand adverse events.

Conclusion:

Actuarial principles and methodologies provide insurance companies with powerful tools for assessing, pricing, and managing risks in insurance portfolios. By leveraging probability theory, statistical analysis, survival analysis, risk modeling, and financial mathematics, actuaries can quantify the likelihood and impact of future events, develop pricing models, and establish risk management strategies to protect policyholders and ensure the financial stability of insurance companies. Actuarial science continues to evolve with advances in data analytics, machine learning, and predictive modeling, enabling actuaries to enhance their risk assessment capabilities and address emerging risks in the insurance industry effectively. In the chapters to come, we will explore advanced techniques and innovations in actuarial science, further deepening our understanding of risk assessment and management in the insurance industry.

Chapter: Reinsurance Strategies to Manage Catastrophic Risk

Catastrophic events, such as natural disasters, large-scale accidents, and pandemics, pose significant financial risks to insurance companies, potentially leading to substantial losses and impairing their ability to meet policyholder obligations. Reinsurance plays a critical role in helping insurance companies manage catastrophic risk by transferring a portion of their risk exposure to other insurers or reinsurers. In this chapter, we explore various reinsurance strategies and mechanisms used by insurance companies to mitigate catastrophic risk effectively.

Traditional Reinsurance:

Traditional reinsurance involves transferring a portion of insurance risk to reinsurers in exchange for payment of premiums. Insurance companies purchase reinsurance coverage to protect against large or catastrophic losses that exceed their risk tolerance or capital capacity. Reinsurance contracts may cover specific lines of business, geographical regions, or per-occurrence and aggregate limits. Traditional reinsurance arrangements include:

Excess of Loss (XOL) Reinsurance: XOL reinsurance provides coverage for losses exceeding a predetermined retention level, known as the "attachment point." Insurance companies retain a portion of the risk up to the retention level and cede the excess risk to reinsurers. XOL reinsurance is commonly used to protect against large individual losses or catastrophic events.

Quota Share Reinsurance: Quota share reinsurance involves ceding a fixed percentage of insurance premiums and losses to reinsurers. Under a quota share arrangement, reinsurers assume a predetermined share of the risk for each policy issued by the insurance company. Quota share reinsurance provides proportional coverage for all policies written by the insurance company.

Stop-Loss Reinsurance: Stop-loss reinsurance, also known as aggregate excess of loss reinsurance, provides coverage for losses exceeding a specified aggregate limit over a policy period. Stop-loss reinsurance protects insurance companies against adverse loss experience or accumulation of losses across multiple policies within a defined period.

Catastrophe Reinsurance:

Catastrophe reinsurance, or cat reinsurance, is specifically designed to protect insurance companies against large-scale catastrophic events, such as hurricanes, earthquakes, wildfires, and terrorist attacks. Catastrophe reinsurance provides coverage for losses resulting from multiple events within a defined geographical area or peril. Catastrophe reinsurance structures include:

Catastrophe Bonds (Cat Bonds): Cat bonds are financial instruments issued by insurance companies or special-purpose vehicles (SPVs) to transfer catastrophic risk to capital markets investors. Cat bonds provide insurance companies with protection against catastrophic losses by paying investors a coupon during the bond's term and using the proceeds to cover losses in the event of a specified catastrophe.

Industry Loss Warranties (ILWs): ILWs are reinsurance contracts that pay out based on industry-wide losses resulting from catastrophic events. ILWs provide coverage for losses exceeding a predefined industry loss threshold, such as insured losses from hurricanes, earthquakes, or other natural disasters. ILWs are used by insurance companies to hedge against systemic catastrophe risk and protect their balance sheets.

Parametric Reinsurance: Parametric reinsurance contracts pay out based on predefined triggers, such as wind speed, earthquake magnitude, or rainfall intensity, rather than actual losses incurred by the insured. Parametric reinsurance provides rapid and transparent coverage for catastrophic events, allowing insurance companies to respond quickly to policyholder claims and reduce claims processing time.

Strategic Partnerships and Alternative Risk Transfer:

In addition to traditional reinsurance structures, insurance companies may engage in strategic partnerships and alternative risk transfer mechanisms to manage catastrophic risk effectively. Strategic partnerships with government agencies, international organizations, and non-profit entities can provide additional support and financial assistance in the event of large-scale disasters. Alternative risk transfer solutions, such as captive insurance companies, risk pools, and collateralized reinsurance, offer innovative approaches to risk financing and risk sharing.

Conclusion:

Reinsurance is a vital tool for insurance companies to manage catastrophic risk effectively and protect their financial stability in the face of large-scale disasters. By transferring a portion of their risk exposure to reinsurers, insurance companies can enhance their capacity to absorb losses, maintain solvency, and meet policyholder obligations. Traditional reinsurance structures, catastrophe reinsurance solutions, and alternative risk transfer mechanisms offer a range of options for insurance companies to diversify risk, optimize capital efficiency, and mitigate catastrophic risk effectively. In the chapters to come, we will explore advanced reinsurance strategies, emerging trends, and innovations in catastrophic risk management, further enhancing our understanding of reinsurance practices in the insurance industry.

Chapter: Regulatory Considerations and Solvency Requirements for Insurers

Regulatory oversight plays a crucial role in ensuring the stability, integrity, and solvency of the insurance industry. Regulatory bodies establish rules, standards, and guidelines to govern the operations, financial management, and risk-taking activities of insurance companies, protecting policyholders and maintaining confidence in the insurance marketplace. In this chapter, we explore the regulatory considerations and solvency requirements imposed on insurers to promote sound risk management practices, financial stability, and consumer protection.

Regulatory Framework:

The regulatory framework for insurers varies by jurisdiction and is typically overseen by government agencies or regulatory authorities responsible for insurance supervision. Regulatory bodies establish laws, regulations, and licensing requirements to govern the formation, licensing, and operation of insurance companies. Key aspects of the regulatory framework for insurers include:

Licensing and Authorization: Insurance companies must obtain regulatory approval and licensing to operate legally within a jurisdiction. Regulatory authorities evaluate the financial strength, management competence, and business viability of insurance companies before granting authorization to conduct insurance business.

Financial Reporting and Disclosure: Insurers are required to comply with regulatory reporting and disclosure requirements, providing transparent and timely financial information to regulatory authorities, policyholders, and other stakeholders. Regulatory reporting standards, such as International Financial Reporting Standards (IFRS) or Generally Accepted Accounting Principles (GAAP), govern the preparation and presentation of financial statements by insurers.

Capital Adequacy and Solvency: Regulatory authorities establish capital adequacy and solvency requirements to ensure that insurance companies maintain sufficient capital reserves to cover policyholder obligations and withstand adverse events. Solvency regulations impose minimum capital standards, risk-based capital (RBC) ratios, and solvency margins to safeguard the financial stability and solvency of insurers.

Solvency Regulation:

Solvency regulation is designed to assess and monitor the financial strength and solvency of insurance companies, ensuring that they have adequate capital to meet policyholder obligations and absorb unexpected losses. Solvency regulation encompasses various quantitative and qualitative measures to evaluate the financial condition and risk profile of insurers. Key components of solvency regulation include:

Risk-Based Capital (RBC) Framework: Risk-based capital (RBC) frameworks assess the capital adequacy of insurance companies based on the risks inherent in their operations, including underwriting risk, investment risk, credit risk, liquidity risk, and operational risk. RBC ratios measure the relationship between regulatory capital and risk exposures, providing insights into insurers' solvency positions.

Solvency II: Solvency II is a comprehensive regulatory framework introduced by the European Union (EU) to harmonize solvency regulation and risk management practices across European insurers. Solvency II establishes requirements for capital adequacy, risk assessment, governance, and reporting, aiming to enhance the financial stability and resilience of insurance companies operating in the EU.

Own Risk and Solvency Assessment (ORSA): Own Risk and Solvency Assessment (ORSA) is a risk management process mandated by regulators to assess insurers' overall solvency positions, identify key risks, and evaluate capital adequacy under various stress scenarios. ORSA requires insurers to conduct regular assessments of their risk profiles, capital requirements, and solvency positions, integrating risk management into strategic decision-making processes.

Consumer Protection and Market Conduct:

Regulatory oversight extends beyond financial solvency to encompass consumer protection and market conduct standards, ensuring fair treatment of policyholders and maintaining confidence in the insurance marketplace. Regulatory authorities enforce laws and regulations related to product suitability, sales practices, claims handling, advertising, and dispute resolution. Regulatory compliance ensures that insurers act in the best interests of policyholders, provide clear and accurate information, and uphold high standards of professionalism and ethical conduct.

Conclusion:

Regulatory considerations and solvency requirements are fundamental to the governance and operation of the insurance industry, promoting financial stability, consumer protection, and market integrity. Regulatory oversight ensures that insurance companies adhere to prudential standards, maintain adequate capital reserves, and manage risks effectively to protect policyholders and meet their contractual obligations. By establishing clear regulatory frameworks, supervisory authorities contribute to the stability and resilience of the insurance sector, fostering trust and confidence in the insurance marketplace. In the chapters to come, we will explore emerging regulatory trends, regulatory compliance challenges, and innovations in insurance regulation, further deepening our understanding of the regulatory landscape for insurers.

Chapter: Risk Management in the Finance Industry: Risk Management Practices in Banking and Financial Institutions

Risk management is a cornerstone of the finance industry, essential for ensuring the stability, resilience, and profitability of banking and financial institutions. With the complexity and interconnectedness of financial markets, institutions face a diverse range of risks, including credit risk, market risk, liquidity risk, operational risk, and regulatory risk. In this chapter, we explore the risk management practices adopted by banking and financial institutions to identify, assess, mitigate, and monitor risks effectively.

Credit Risk Management:

Credit risk, also known as default risk, arises from the possibility that borrowers may fail to repay their debts or obligations as agreed. Banking and financial institutions employ robust credit risk management practices to assess the creditworthiness of borrowers, mitigate potential losses, and maintain healthy loan portfolios. Key aspects of credit risk management include:

Credit Underwriting: Institutions conduct thorough credit underwriting processes to evaluate the financial health, repayment capacity, and creditworthiness of borrowers. Underwriting criteria may include credit scores, income verification, collateral valuation, and debt-to-income ratios.

Credit Risk Assessment: Institutions employ quantitative models, credit scoring systems, and credit rating methodologies to assess the probability of default and loss severity associated with lending activities. Credit risk assessment helps institutions quantify and manage credit exposures across different borrower segments and loan portfolios.

Credit Monitoring and Review: Institutions continuously monitor credit exposures, loan performance, and credit quality indicators to identify early warning signs of deteriorating credit conditions. Regular credit reviews, loan portfolio stress testing, and credit risk analytics enable institutions to proactively manage credit risk and take timely risk mitigation actions.

Market Risk Management:

Market risk, also known as price risk, arises from fluctuations in financial market prices, including interest rates, foreign exchange rates, equity prices, and commodity prices. Banking and financial institutions implement robust market risk management practices to quantify, hedge, and monitor market exposures effectively. Key aspects of market risk management include:

Risk Measurement: Institutions employ quantitative models, such as value-at-risk (VaR) models, stress testing, and scenario analysis, to measure and assess market risk exposures across trading, investment, and banking activities. Risk measures provide insights into potential losses and volatility under different market conditions.

Hedging Strategies: Institutions use derivatives, options, futures, and other financial instruments to hedge market exposures and mitigate potential losses arising from adverse market movements. Hedging strategies, such as interest rate swaps, currency forwards, and options strategies, help institutions manage interest rate risk, currency risk, and commodity price risk.

Portfolio Diversification: Institutions diversify their investment portfolios across different asset classes, sectors, and geographic regions to reduce concentration risk and minimize exposure to specific market risks. Portfolio diversification strategies help institutions optimize risk-adjusted returns and mitigate the impact of adverse market events.

Liquidity Risk Management:

Liquidity risk arises from the inability of institutions to meet their short-term funding obligations or liquidate assets at fair market value without incurring significant losses. Liquidity risk management practices focus on maintaining adequate liquidity buffers, managing cash flows, and diversifying funding sources to withstand liquidity shocks. Key aspects of liquidity risk management include:

Liquidity Stress Testing: Institutions conduct liquidity stress tests and scenario analysis to assess their ability to withstand liquidity disruptions and funding shortfalls under adverse market conditions. Stress testing helps institutions identify potential liquidity gaps, funding mismatches, and liquidity risk concentrations.

Contingency Funding Plans: Institutions develop contingency funding plans (CFPs) and liquidity risk management frameworks to outline strategies for accessing emergency funding sources, such as central bank facilities, interbank markets, and emergency liquidity facilities. CFPs specify the procedures and actions to be taken in response to liquidity stress events.

Asset-Liability Management (ALM): Institutions employ asset-liability management (ALM) techniques to match the maturities, cash flows, and interest rate sensitivities of assets and liabilities, minimizing liquidity risk and funding mismatches. ALM strategies optimize the composition of balance sheets, funding structures, and liquidity reserves to enhance liquidity management and risk mitigation.

Operational Risk Management:

Operational risk arises from internal processes, systems, human errors, and external events that may disrupt business operations, lead to financial losses, or damage reputation. Operational risk management practices focus on identifying, assessing, and mitigating operational risks through effective controls, governance, and risk management frameworks. Key aspects of operational risk management include:

Risk Identification: Institutions conduct risk assessments, business impact analyses, and scenario analyses to identify and prioritize operational risks across various business units, processes, and systems. Risk identification techniques, such as key risk indicators (KRIs) and loss event data analysis, help institutions understand the nature and magnitude of operational risks.

Control Frameworks: Institutions implement robust internal controls, policies, and procedures to mitigate operational risks and prevent control failures, errors, or misconduct. Control frameworks encompass risk management policies, segregation of duties, authorization limits, and compliance with regulatory requirements.

Business Continuity Planning: Institutions develop business continuity plans (BCPs) and disaster recovery plans to ensure the continuity of critical business operations and services in the event of operational disruptions, natural disasters, or other emergencies. BCPs outline procedures for data backup, alternate processing sites, crisis communication, and recovery strategies to minimize downtime and mitigate operational impacts.

Regulatory Risk Management:

Regulatory risk arises from changes in laws, regulations, or government policies that may impact the operations, compliance, and financial performance of institutions. Regulatory risk management practices focus on monitoring regulatory developments, assessing compliance requirements, and implementing controls to mitigate regulatory risks effectively. Key aspects of regulatory risk management include:

Compliance Monitoring: Institutions establish compliance monitoring programs and regulatory risk assessment processes to ensure adherence to applicable laws, regulations, and regulatory guidelines. Compliance monitoring involves conducting regular compliance audits, reviews, and assessments to identify potential regulatory gaps or violations.

Regulatory Reporting: Institutions prepare and submit regulatory reports, disclosures, and filings to regulatory authorities in accordance with regulatory requirements and deadlines. Regulatory reporting ensures transparency, accuracy, and completeness of financial information, risk metrics, and compliance disclosures.

Regulatory Engagement: Institutions engage with regulatory authorities, industry associations, and policymakers to stay informed about regulatory developments, participate in regulatory consultations, and advocate for favorable regulatory outcomes. Regulatory engagement fosters collaboration, dialogue, and constructive feedback between institutions and regulatory stakeholders.

Conclusion:

Risk management is integral to the operations, financial stability, and resilience of banking and financial institutions, enabling them to identify, assess, mitigate, and monitor risks effectively in a dynamic and interconnected financial landscape. Credit risk management, market risk management, liquidity risk management, operational risk management, and regulatory risk management are fundamental pillars of risk management practices in the finance industry. By implementing robust risk management frameworks, controls, and governance structures, institutions can enhance their risk management capabilities, safeguard their financial soundness, and maintain trust and confidence among stakeholders. In the chapters to come, we will explore advanced risk management techniques, emerging risk trends, and innovations in risk management practices in the finance industry.

Chapter: Credit Risk Assessment and Mitigation Techniques

Credit risk, also known as default risk, is one of the primary risks faced by banking and financial institutions, arising from the potential failure of borrowers to meet their debt obligations. Effective credit risk assessment and mitigation are essential for ensuring the financial stability and profitability of institutions, as well as maintaining healthy loan portfolios. In this chapter, we explore the methods and techniques used by institutions to assess, manage, and mitigate credit risk effectively.

Credit Risk Assessment:

Credit risk assessment involves evaluating the creditworthiness of borrowers and assessing the likelihood of default on loan obligations. Institutions employ a range of quantitative and qualitative methods to analyze borrower credit profiles, financial health, and repayment capacity. Key aspects of credit risk assessment include:

Credit Scoring Models: Institutions use credit scoring models to evaluate the creditworthiness of borrowers based on factors such as credit history, income level, debt-to-income ratio, employment status, and asset ownership. Credit scores provide a standardized measure of credit risk and help institutions make informed lending decisions.

Financial Statement Analysis: Institutions analyze borrower financial statements, including income statements, balance sheets, and cash flow statements, to assess financial health, liquidity, solvency, and debt servicing capacity. Financial statement analysis helps institutions identify red flags, such as deteriorating financial performance, excessive leverage, or liquidity constraints.

Collateral Valuation: Institutions may require borrowers to provide collateral, such as real estate, inventory, equipment, or securities, to secure loans and mitigate credit risk. Collateral valuation involves assessing the market value, liquidity, and quality of collateral assets to determine their adequacy in covering loan exposures.

Cash Flow Analysis: Institutions analyze borrower cash flows, cash flow projections, and debt service coverage ratios (DSCR) to assess the ability to generate sufficient cash flow to service debt obligations. Cash flow analysis helps institutions evaluate repayment capacity and identify potential liquidity constraints or cash flow mismatches.

Credit Risk Mitigation Techniques:

Once credit risk is assessed, institutions employ various techniques to mitigate and manage credit risk exposures effectively. Credit risk mitigation techniques aim to reduce the likelihood of default, minimize potential losses, and protect institutions' financial interests. Key credit risk mitigation techniques include:

Diversification: Institutions diversify their loan portfolios across different borrower segments, industries, geographic regions, and loan types to reduce concentration risk and minimize exposure to specific credit risks. Diversification spreads risk and enhances portfolio resilience against adverse events or economic downturns.

Credit Enhancement: Institutions use credit enhancement techniques to improve the credit quality of loans and enhance borrower creditworthiness. Credit enhancement mechanisms include guarantees, collateralization, insurance, letters of credit, and third-party credit enhancements, which provide additional protection against default risk.

Loan Structuring: Institutions structure loans with appropriate terms, covenants, and repayment schedules to mitigate credit risk and align with borrower cash flows and repayment capacity. Loan structuring techniques include establishing loan-to-value (LTV) ratios, debt service coverage ratios (DSCR), loan maturities, and amortization schedules tailored to borrower needs and risk profiles.

Risk Transfer: Institutions transfer credit risk exposures to third parties through securitization, credit derivatives, loan sales, and syndication arrangements. Risk transfer mechanisms allow institutions to offload credit risk to investors, reinsurers, or counterparties, reducing exposure to potential losses and freeing up capital for new lending activities.

Credit Monitoring and Surveillance: Institutions implement robust credit monitoring and surveillance processes to track borrower credit performance, monitor loan portfolios, and identify early warning signs of deteriorating credit conditions. Credit monitoring involves regular credit reviews, borrower communication, financial statement analysis, and risk rating updates to proactively manage credit risk exposures.

Conclusion:

Credit risk assessment and mitigation are critical components of effective risk management practices in banking and financial institutions, essential for protecting institutions' financial stability, profitability, and reputation. By employing rigorous credit risk assessment methodologies and implementing prudent credit risk mitigation techniques, institutions can identify, evaluate, and manage credit risk exposures effectively. Diversification, credit enhancement, loan structuring, risk transfer, and credit monitoring are essential tools for mitigating credit risk and safeguarding institutions' loan portfolios against default events. In the chapters to come, we will explore advanced credit risk management techniques, emerging trends, and innovations in credit risk assessment and mitigation practices.

Chapter: Market Risk Management in Trading and Investment Activities

Market risk, also known as price risk, is inherent in trading and investment activities and arises from fluctuations in financial market prices, including interest rates, foreign exchange rates, equity prices, commodity prices, and volatility levels. Effective market risk management is essential for financial institutions, investment firms, and traders to protect capital, optimize risk-adjusted returns, and preserve financial stability. In this chapter, we explore the methods and techniques used to identify, assess, and manage market risk in trading and investment activities.

Types of Market Risk:

Market risk encompasses various types of risks that can affect the value of financial instruments and investment portfolios. The primary types of market risk include:

Interest Rate Risk: Interest rate risk arises from changes in interest rates, affecting the value of fixed-income securities, bond portfolios, and interest-sensitive financial instruments. Fluctuations in interest rates impact bond prices, yield curves, and duration characteristics, leading to potential gains or losses for investors.

Foreign Exchange Risk: Foreign exchange risk arises from fluctuations in currency exchange rates, impacting the value of international investments, foreign currency positions, and cross-border transactions. Changes in exchange rates affect the competitiveness of exports and imports, corporate earnings, and translation of foreign currency-denominated assets and liabilities.

Equity Price Risk: Equity price risk arises from changes in stock prices, affecting the value of equity investments, stock portfolios, and equity derivatives. Volatility in equity markets can result from macroeconomic factors, company-specific news, geopolitical events, or investor sentiment, leading to potential gains or losses for equity investors.

Commodity Price Risk: Commodity price risk arises from fluctuations in commodity prices, impacting the value of commodity investments, commodity derivatives, and commodity-related assets. Changes in supply and demand dynamics, geopolitical tensions, weather patterns, and global economic conditions influence commodity prices and volatility levels.

Market Risk Management Techniques:

Market risk management techniques aim to identify, assess, and mitigate market risk exposures in trading and investment activities. Key market risk management techniques include:

Risk Measurement: Institutions use quantitative models, risk metrics, and analytics tools to measure and quantify market risk exposures across trading and investment portfolios. Risk measures such as value-at-risk (VaR), expected shortfall (ES), and stress testing provide insights into potential losses and volatility under different market scenarios.

Portfolio Diversification: Investors diversify their investment portfolios across different asset classes, sectors, regions, and investment strategies to reduce concentration risk and minimize exposure to specific market risks. Portfolio diversification spreads risk and enhances portfolio resilience against adverse market events or economic downturns.

Hedging Strategies: Investors use hedging strategies, such as options, futures, swaps, and other derivatives, to offset or mitigate market risk exposures in their portfolios. Hedging techniques help investors protect against adverse price movements, volatility spikes, or unexpected events by establishing offsetting positions or insurance-like instruments.

Asset Allocation: Investors employ strategic asset allocation strategies to allocate capital to different asset classes based on risk-return objectives, investment horizon, and market outlook. Asset allocation decisions balance risk and return considerations, optimizing portfolio construction and risk-adjusted returns.

Stop-loss Orders: Traders use stop-loss orders and risk management rules to limit potential losses and control downside risk in trading positions. Stop-loss orders automatically trigger the sale of assets or closing of positions when prices reach predefined levels, helping traders manage risk and preserve capital.

Conclusion:

Market risk management is essential for financial institutions, investment firms, and traders to navigate the complexities of financial markets, protect capital, and achieve investment objectives. Interest rate risk, foreign exchange risk, equity price risk, and commodity price risk are primary types of market risk that can impact the value of trading and investment portfolios. Market risk management techniques, such as risk measurement, portfolio diversification, hedging strategies, asset allocation, and stop-loss orders, help institutions and investors identify, assess, and mitigate market risk exposures effectively. By implementing robust market risk management practices, institutions and investors can optimize risk-adjusted returns, preserve capital, and maintain resilience in the face of market uncertainties. In the chapters to come, we will explore advanced market risk management techniques, emerging trends, and innovations in trading and investment activities.

Chapter: Operational Risk Management and Compliance Frameworks

Operational risk management and compliance frameworks are integral components of sound governance practices in financial institutions and organizations. Operational risk arises from internal processes, systems, human errors, and external events that may disrupt business operations, lead to financial losses, or damage reputation. Effective operational risk management and compliance frameworks help institutions identify, assess, mitigate, and monitor operational risks, ensuring regulatory compliance, operational resilience, and business continuity. In this chapter, we explore the methods and techniques used to establish operational risk management and compliance frameworks.

Operational Risk Management:

Operational risk management involves identifying, assessing, mitigating, and monitoring operational risks across various business functions, processes, and systems within an organization. Key aspects of operational risk management include:

Risk Identification: Organizations conduct risk assessments, business impact analyses, and scenario analyses to identify and prioritize operational risks, including process failures, system outages, human errors, fraud, and cybersecurity threats. Risk identification techniques, such as key risk indicators (KRIs), risk control self-assessments (RCSAs), and loss event data analysis, help organizations understand the nature and magnitude of operational risks.

Risk Assessment: Organizations assess the likelihood and impact of operational risks using qualitative and quantitative methods, such as risk matrices, risk heat maps, and risk quantification models. Risk assessment techniques help organizations prioritize risk mitigation efforts, allocate resources effectively, and develop risk management strategies tailored to specific risk profiles.

Risk Mitigation: Organizations implement risk mitigation measures, controls, and remediation plans to reduce the likelihood and severity of operational risk events. Risk mitigation strategies may include process improvements, automation, segregation of duties, access controls, training and awareness programs, and incident response protocols. Risk mitigation efforts aim to strengthen internal controls, prevent control failures, and enhance operational resilience.

Risk Monitoring and Reporting: Organizations establish robust risk monitoring and reporting mechanisms to track operational risk exposures, control effectiveness, and risk mitigation progress. Regular risk monitoring involves monitoring key risk indicators (KRIs), control testing results, and incident reports to identify emerging risks, control deficiencies, and areas requiring remediation. Risk reporting provides stakeholders, senior management, and regulators with transparency and insights into operational risk profiles, trends, and control effectiveness.

Compliance Frameworks:

Compliance frameworks encompass policies, procedures, controls, and governance structures designed to ensure adherence to applicable laws, regulations, standards, and ethical principles. Key aspects of compliance frameworks include:

Regulatory Compliance: Organizations establish regulatory compliance programs to comply with laws, regulations, and regulatory requirements applicable to their industry, jurisdiction, and business activities. Regulatory compliance programs encompass regulatory monitoring, interpretation of regulatory requirements, compliance risk assessments, and implementation of controls to mitigate compliance risks.

Policy and Procedure Management: Organizations develop and maintain policies, procedures, and guidelines to establish clear expectations, standards, and controls for conducting business operations in compliance with regulatory requirements and internal policies. Policy and procedure management includes policy development, approval, dissemination, training, enforcement, and periodic review to ensure alignment with regulatory standards and industry best practices.

Compliance Training and Awareness: Organizations provide compliance training and awareness programs to educate employees, managers, and stakeholders about regulatory requirements, ethical standards, and compliance obligations. Compliance training programs cover topics such as anti-money laundering (AML), know your customer (KYC), data privacy, insider trading, and ethical conduct, fostering a culture of compliance and ethical behavior within the organization.

Compliance Monitoring and Testing: Organizations conduct compliance monitoring, testing, and internal audits to evaluate the effectiveness of compliance controls, identify compliance gaps, and assess adherence to regulatory requirements. Compliance monitoring involves conducting periodic reviews, testing controls, and assessing compliance with regulatory standards, policies, and procedures. Internal audits provide independent assurance and recommendations for improving compliance processes and controls.

Regulatory Reporting and Disclosure: Organizations prepare and submit regulatory reports, filings, and disclosures to regulatory authorities in accordance with regulatory requirements and deadlines. Regulatory reporting encompasses financial reporting, regulatory filings, compliance attestations, and disclosures of material information to regulators, investors, and stakeholders.

Conclusion:

Operational risk management and compliance frameworks are essential components of effective governance, risk management, and control practices in organizations. Operational risk management involves identifying, assessing, mitigating, and monitoring operational risks across business functions, processes, and systems to ensure operational resilience and business continuity. Compliance frameworks establish policies, procedures, controls, and governance structures to ensure adherence to applicable laws, regulations, and ethical standards. By implementing robust operational risk management and compliance frameworks, organizations can enhance operational efficiency, regulatory compliance, and stakeholder trust. In the chapters to come, we will explore advanced operational risk management techniques, emerging compliance trends, and innovations in governance and control practices.

Chapter: Financial Risk Management: Overview and Objectives

Financial risk management is a critical component of strategic decision-making and operational activities in organizations, encompassing the identification, assessment, mitigation, and monitoring of risks that may impact financial performance, cash flows, and capital adequacy. Effective financial risk management helps organizations optimize risk-return trade-offs, protect against adverse events, and enhance resilience in dynamic and uncertain financial environments. In this chapter, we provide an overview of financial risk management and discuss its objectives.

Overview of Financial Risk Management:

Financial risk management involves the identification, assessment, mitigation, and monitoring of risks that may affect an organization's financial health, profitability, and value creation. Financial risks can arise from various sources, including market volatility, credit defaults, liquidity constraints, operational disruptions, regulatory changes, and external macroeconomic factors. Key categories of financial risk include:

Market Risk: Market risk arises from fluctuations in financial market prices, including interest rates, foreign exchange rates, equity prices, commodity prices, and volatility levels. Market risk affects the value of investment portfolios, trading positions, and financial assets, leading to potential gains or losses for organizations.

Credit Risk: Credit risk, also known as default risk, arises from the possibility that borrowers may fail to fulfill their debt obligations or default on loan repayments. Credit risk impacts the quality of loan portfolios, debt securities, and credit exposures, affecting the financial stability and profitability of lending institutions and investors.

Liquidity Risk: Liquidity risk arises from the inability of organizations to meet their short-term funding obligations or liquidate assets at fair market value without incurring significant losses. Liquidity risk affects the ability of organizations to access funding sources, manage cash flows, and withstand liquidity shocks or funding disruptions.

Operational Risk: Operational risk arises from internal processes, systems, human errors, and external events that may disrupt business operations, lead to financial losses, or damage reputation. Operational risk impacts the efficiency, resilience, and reputation of organizations, requiring robust controls, governance, and risk management practices.

Objectives of Financial Risk Management:

The primary objectives of financial risk management are to:

Identify Risks: Financial risk management aims to identify and assess risks that may impact an organization's financial performance, cash flows, and capital adequacy. By understanding the nature, magnitude, and drivers of financial risks, organizations can prioritize risk mitigation efforts and allocate resources effectively.

Assess Risks: Financial risk management involves assessing the likelihood and potential impact of risks on organizational objectives, financial metrics, and stakeholder interests. Risk assessment techniques, such as quantitative models, stress testing, scenario analysis, and risk mapping, help organizations quantify and prioritize risks based on their severity and frequency.

Mitigate Risks: Financial risk management aims to mitigate and control risks through appropriate risk mitigation measures, controls, and risk transfer mechanisms. Risk mitigation strategies may include diversification, hedging, insurance, reinsurance, capital buffers, and operational controls, tailored to specific risk exposures and risk appetite.

Monitor Risks: Financial risk management involves monitoring and tracking risk exposures, control effectiveness, and risk mitigation progress over time. Regular risk monitoring, key risk indicators (KRIs), control self-assessments (CSAs), and risk reporting enable organizations to identify emerging risks, control deficiencies, and areas requiring remediation.

Conclusion:

Financial risk management is essential for organizations to navigate the complexities of financial markets, protect against adverse events, and achieve strategic objectives. Market risk, credit risk, liquidity risk, and operational risk are primary categories of financial risk that organizations must identify, assess, mitigate, and monitor effectively. By implementing robust financial risk management practices, organizations can optimize risk-return trade-offs, protect against downside risks, and enhance resilience in dynamic and uncertain financial environments. In the chapters to come, we will explore advanced financial risk management techniques, emerging risk trends, and innovations in risk management practices.

Chapter: Hedging Strategies for Managing Currency Risk, Interest Rate Risk, and Commodity Price Risk

Hedging is a risk management technique used by organizations to mitigate the impact of adverse price movements on financial instruments or commodities. Hedging strategies enable organizations to protect against currency risk, interest rate risk, and commodity price risk by establishing offsetting positions or insurance-like instruments. In this chapter, we explore hedging strategies tailored to managing currency risk, interest rate risk, and commodity price risk.

Hedging Currency Risk:

Currency risk, also known as foreign exchange risk, arises from fluctuations in currency exchange rates, impacting the value of international investments, foreign currency positions, and cross-border transactions. Hedging currency risk involves using financial instruments to offset or mitigate the impact of adverse currency movements. Common hedging strategies for managing currency risk include:

Forward Contracts: Forward contracts are agreements to buy or sell a specified amount of currency at a predetermined exchange rate on a future date. Organizations use forward contracts to lock in exchange rates and eliminate uncertainty in future cash flows or transaction costs associated with foreign currency-denominated assets, liabilities, or revenues.

Currency Options: Currency options provide organizations with the right, but not the obligation, to buy (call option) or sell (put option) a specified amount of currency at a predetermined exchange rate within a specified period. Organizations use currency options to hedge against adverse currency movements while retaining flexibility in currency exchange decisions.

Currency Swaps: Currency swaps involve exchanging cash flows in different currencies over a specified period, allowing organizations to hedge currency risk and manage currency exposures effectively. Organizations use currency swaps to convert foreign currency cash flows into their domestic currency or vice versa, mitigating exchange rate volatility and minimizing transaction costs.

Hedging Interest Rate Risk:

Interest rate risk arises from fluctuations in interest rates, impacting the value of fixed-income securities, bond portfolios, and interest-sensitive financial instruments. Hedging interest rate risk involves using financial instruments to protect against adverse interest rate movements and stabilize cash flows. Common hedging strategies for managing interest rate risk include:

Interest Rate Swaps: Interest rate swaps involve exchanging fixed-rate and floating-rate cash flows over a specified period, allowing organizations to hedge against interest rate fluctuations and manage interest rate exposures. Organizations use interest rate swaps to lock in fixed interest rates or convert floating-rate cash flows into fixed-rate cash flows, reducing interest rate risk.

Interest Rate Futures: Interest rate futures are standardized contracts to buy or sell fixed-income securities or interest rate instruments at a predetermined price and date in the future. Organizations use interest rate futures to hedge against changes in interest rates, adjust portfolio duration, or replicate exposure to specific segments of the yield curve.

Interest Rate Options: Interest rate options provide organizations with the right, but not the obligation, to buy (call option) or sell (put option) interest rate futures contracts or fixed-income securities at a predetermined price within a specified period. Organizations use interest rate options to hedge against adverse interest rate movements while retaining flexibility in interest rate risk management.

Hedging Commodity Price Risk:

Commodity price risk arises from fluctuations in commodity prices, impacting the value of commodity investments, commodity derivatives, and commodity-related assets. Hedging commodity price risk involves using financial instruments to protect against adverse commodity price movements and stabilize cash flows. Common hedging strategies for managing commodity price risk include:

Commodity Futures: Commodity futures are standardized contracts to buy or sell a specified quantity of a commodity at a predetermined price and date in the future. Organizations use commodity futures to hedge against changes in commodity prices, lock in prices for future delivery, or manage exposure to specific commodity markets.

Commodity Options: Commodity options provide organizations with the right, but not the obligation, to buy (call option) or sell (put option) commodity futures contracts or physical commodities at a predetermined price within a specified period. Organizations use commodity options to hedge against adverse commodity price movements while retaining flexibility in commodity price risk management.

Commodity Swaps: Commodity swaps involve exchanging cash flows based on commodity prices over a specified period, allowing organizations to hedge commodity price risk and manage commodity exposures effectively. Organizations use commodity swaps to lock in prices for future commodity deliveries, hedge production or consumption risks, and stabilize cash flows.

Conclusion:

Hedging strategies are essential tools for organizations to manage currency risk, interest rate risk, and commodity price risk effectively. Forward contracts, currency options, and currency swaps are common hedging instruments used to mitigate currency risk, stabilize foreign currency cash flows, and manage currency exposures. Interest rate swaps, interest rate futures, and interest rate options are prevalent hedging instruments used to hedge interest rate risk, stabilize fixed-income portfolios, and manage interest rate exposures. Commodity futures, commodity options, and commodity swaps are widely used hedging instruments to hedge commodity price risk, stabilize commodity-related cash flows, and manage exposure to commodity markets. By implementing appropriate hedging strategies, organizations can reduce risk, protect against adverse price movements, and enhance financial resilience in dynamic and uncertain markets. In the chapters to come, we will explore advanced hedging techniques, emerging trends, and innovations in risk management practices.

Chapter: Derivative Instruments and Their Role in Risk Management

Introduction:

Derivative instruments are financial contracts whose value derives from the performance of an underlying asset, index, or variable. Derivatives serve various purposes in financial markets, including risk management, speculation, and hedging. In this chapter, we explore derivative instruments and their critical role in risk management.

Understanding Derivative Instruments:

Derivative instruments come in various forms, including futures contracts, forward contracts, options, swaps, and structured products. Each derivative type serves specific purposes and provides unique risk management opportunities. Here's a brief overview:

Futures Contracts: Futures contracts obligate the buyer to purchase, and the seller to sell, a specified asset at a predetermined price (the futures price) on a future date. Futures contracts are standardized and traded on exchanges, providing liquidity and transparency. They are commonly used for hedging and speculation in commodities, currencies, interest rates, and equity indices.

Forward Contracts: Forward contracts are similar to futures contracts but are customized agreements between two parties to buy or sell an asset at a specified price (the forward price) on a future date. Forward contracts are traded over the counter (OTC) and are tailored to meet specific hedging needs. They are commonly used for hedging foreign exchange risk, interest rate risk, and commodity price risk.

Options: Options provide the buyer with the right, but not the obligation, to buy (call option) or sell (put option) an asset at a predetermined price (the strike price) within a specified period (the option's expiration). Options offer flexibility and asymmetrical risk profiles, making them valuable for hedging, speculation, and managing downside risk. They are commonly used for hedging equity risk, currency risk, and interest rate risk.

Swaps: Swaps are agreements between two parties to exchange cash flows or liabilities based on predetermined terms over a specified period. Common types of swaps include interest rate swaps, currency swaps, and commodity swaps. Swaps are versatile instruments used for hedging, arbitrage, and managing cash flow mismatches. They provide tailored solutions for managing interest rate risk, currency risk, and commodity price risk.

Role of Derivatives in Risk Management:

Derivative instruments play a vital role in risk management by allowing market participants to transfer, hedge, or mitigate various types of financial risks. Some key roles of derivatives in risk management include:

Hedging: Derivatives enable businesses, investors, and financial institutions to hedge against adverse price movements, volatility, and uncertainty in financial markets. By using derivatives strategically, market participants can protect against downside risk, stabilize cash flows, and preserve capital.

Risk Transfer: Derivatives facilitate the transfer of risk from one party to another, allowing entities to offload or share risk exposures with counterparties willing to accept them. Through risk transfer mechanisms such as futures, options, and swaps, market participants can redistribute risk and optimize risk-return profiles.

Portfolio Diversification: Derivatives offer opportunities for portfolio diversification and risk mitigation by providing exposure to different asset classes, markets, and risk factors. By incorporating derivatives into investment portfolios, investors can enhance diversification, reduce correlation risk, and improve portfolio efficiency.

Price Discovery: Derivatives markets serve as important price discovery mechanisms, providing valuable information about the future direction, volatility, and expectations of underlying assets or markets. By analyzing derivatives prices and trading activity, market participants gain insights into market sentiment, supply-demand dynamics, and risk perceptions.

Conclusion:

Derivative instruments play a crucial role in risk management by providing tools for hedging, risk transfer, portfolio diversification, and price discovery. Futures contracts, forward contracts, options, and swaps offer versatile solutions for managing various types of financial risks, including commodity risk, currency risk, interest rate risk, and equity risk. By incorporating derivatives into risk management strategies, businesses, investors, and financial institutions can mitigate risk exposures, optimize risk-return profiles, and navigate volatile and uncertain financial markets effectively. In the chapters to come, we will explore advanced derivative strategies, risk management techniques, and emerging trends in derivatives markets.

Chapter: Effective Risk Management Practices in Real-World Scenarios

Risk management is an essential aspect of decision-making and strategic planning in real-world scenarios, encompassing a wide range of industries, sectors, and organizational contexts. Effective risk management practices enable businesses, governments, and individuals to identify, assess, mitigate, and monitor risks proactively, thereby enhancing resilience, protecting assets, and achieving strategic objectives. In this chapter, we explore effective risk management practices in real-world scenarios and examine their application across various contexts.

Identifying Risks:

Effective risk management begins with identifying and understanding the potential risks that may impact organizational objectives, operations, and stakeholders. In real-world scenarios, risks can arise from internal and external sources, including market volatility, regulatory changes, operational disruptions, cybersecurity threats, natural disasters, and geopolitical events. Organizations employ various methods and techniques to identify risks, such as risk assessments, scenario analyses, SWOT analyses, historical data analysis, and expert judgment. By systematically identifying risks, organizations can prioritize risk management efforts and allocate resources effectively.

Assessing Risks:

Once risks are identified, organizations must assess the likelihood and potential impact of each risk on organizational objectives, financial performance, and stakeholder interests. Risk assessment involves analyzing the probability of occurrence, severity of consequences, interdependencies, and mitigating factors associated with each risk. Quantitative and qualitative methods, such as risk matrices, risk scoring models, Monte Carlo simulations, and sensitivity analyses, are used to assess risks and prioritize them based on their significance and urgency. By conducting comprehensive risk assessments, organizations can develop risk profiles, establish risk tolerances, and inform decision-making processes.

Mitigating Risks:

After assessing risks, organizations implement risk mitigation measures, controls, and strategies to reduce the likelihood and severity of adverse events. Risk mitigation involves taking proactive actions to avoid, minimize, transfer, or accept risks within acceptable limits. Common risk mitigation strategies include implementing internal controls, enhancing cybersecurity measures, diversifying portfolios, purchasing insurance coverage, hedging exposures, improving business processes, and developing contingency plans. By implementing robust risk mitigation measures, organizations can reduce vulnerabilities, protect assets, and enhance resilience to unforeseen events.

Monitoring Risks:

Effective risk management requires ongoing monitoring and surveillance of risks to ensure that mitigation measures remain effective and responsive to changing circumstances. Risk monitoring involves tracking key risk indicators (KRIs), control effectiveness, emerging risks, and risk mitigation progress over time. Regular risk assessments, internal audits, compliance reviews, and incident reporting mechanisms are used to monitor risks and detect early warning signs of potential issues. By maintaining vigilance and responsiveness, organizations can adapt to evolving risk landscapes, mitigate emerging threats, and maintain proactive risk management practices.

Case Studies:

Real-world case studies provide valuable insights into effective risk management practices across different industries and sectors. Examples of successful risk management initiatives include:

Financial institutions implementing stress testing and scenario analysis to assess capital adequacy and liquidity resilience in response to changing market conditions.
Healthcare organizations developing pandemic preparedness plans and supply chain resilience strategies to mitigate risks associated with infectious diseases and global health crises.
Manufacturing companies adopting lean manufacturing principles and just-in-time inventory management to mitigate operational risks and improve efficiency.
Technology firms enhancing cybersecurity protocols and data protection measures to safeguard against cyber threats, data breaches, and information security risks.
Government agencies implementing disaster recovery and business continuity plans to mitigate risks associated with natural disasters, terrorist attacks, and geopolitical instability.
Conclusion:

Effective risk management practices are essential for organizations to navigate uncertainties, protect assets, and achieve strategic objectives in real-world scenarios. By identifying, assessing, mitigating, and monitoring risks proactively, organizations can enhance resilience, optimize risk-return profiles, and create sustainable value for stakeholders. Real-world case studies illustrate the importance of robust risk management practices across different industries and sectors, highlighting the diverse approaches and strategies used to address specific risk challenges. In the chapters to come, we will explore advanced risk management techniques, emerging trends, and best practices in risk management across various contexts.

Chapter: Integrated Risk Management: The Importance of Integration Across an Organization

Integrated risk management (IRM) is a strategic approach that involves coordinating and aligning risk management activities across an organization to enhance decision-making, optimize resource allocation, and improve overall risk resilience. By integrating risk management processes, systems, and capabilities, organizations can gain a comprehensive view of risks, identify interdependencies, and implement holistic risk mitigation strategies. In this chapter, we explore the importance of integrated risk management and its benefits for organizations.

Enhanced Decision-Making:

Integrated risk management enables organizations to make more informed and effective decisions by considering risks across all business functions, processes, and activities. By integrating risk management into decision-making processes, organizations can assess the potential impact of risks on strategic objectives, evaluate risk-reward trade-offs, and identify opportunities to optimize outcomes. Integrated risk assessments provide decision-makers with timely insights into emerging risks, uncertainties, and vulnerabilities, enabling them to make proactive and risk-aware decisions that align with organizational goals and values.

Optimized Resource Allocation:

Integrated risk management helps organizations optimize resource allocation by prioritizing risk mitigation efforts and allocating resources based on risk exposure, significance, and urgency. By centralizing risk data, analytics, and reporting, organizations can identify areas of high-risk concentration, assess the effectiveness of existing controls, and allocate resources to mitigate risks cost-effectively. Integrated risk management enables organizations to align risk management activities with business priorities, strategic initiatives, and performance objectives, ensuring that resources are allocated to areas of greatest impact and value.

Improved Risk Resilience:

Integrated risk management enhances organizational resilience by fostering a proactive and coordinated approach to risk identification, assessment, and mitigation. By integrating risk management processes, organizations can establish a culture of risk awareness, accountability, and transparency across all levels of the organization. Integrated risk management enables organizations to build resilience to unforeseen events, disruptions, and crises by identifying and addressing risks proactively, implementing robust controls and contingency plans, and adapting to changing risk landscapes in real-time.

Streamlined Compliance:

Integrated risk management streamlines compliance efforts by aligning risk management practices with regulatory requirements, industry standards, and best practices. By integrating compliance activities into risk management processes, organizations can identify regulatory obligations, assess compliance risks, and implement controls to mitigate non-compliance risks effectively. Integrated risk management enables organizations to streamline compliance reporting, audits, and assessments by centralizing risk data, documentation, and evidence, thereby reducing duplication of efforts and enhancing regulatory transparency and accountability.

Enhanced Stakeholder Confidence:

Integrated risk management enhances stakeholder confidence by demonstrating a proactive and holistic approach to risk management, governance, and oversight. By integrating risk management practices into corporate governance frameworks, organizations can provide stakeholders with assurance that risks are identified, assessed, and managed effectively to protect value and achieve strategic objectives. Integrated risk management enables organizations to communicate risk information transparently, engage stakeholders in risk discussions, and build trust and credibility with investors, regulators, customers, and other stakeholders.

Conclusion:

Integrated risk management is essential for organizations to enhance decision-making, optimize resource allocation, improve risk resilience, streamline compliance, and enhance stakeholder confidence. By integrating risk management processes, systems, and capabilities across the organization, organizations can gain a comprehensive view of risks, identify interdependencies, and implement holistic risk mitigation strategies that align with business priorities and objectives. In today's complex and dynamic business environment, integrated risk management is critical for organizations to navigate uncertainties, seize opportunities, and create sustainable value for stakeholders. In the chapters to come, we will explore advanced techniques, emerging trends, and best practices in integrated risk management across various industries and sectors.

Chapter: Enterprise Risk Management (ERM) Frameworks and Best Practices

Enterprise Risk Management (ERM) is a strategic approach that enables organizations to identify, assess, mitigate, and monitor risks holistically across all business functions, processes, and activities. ERM frameworks provide a structured methodology for integrating risk management practices into organizational decision-making, governance, and operations. In this chapter, we explore ERM frameworks and best practices that organizations can adopt to enhance risk management effectiveness and resilience.

Understanding ERM Frameworks:

ERM frameworks provide a comprehensive structure for managing risks systematically and proactively throughout an organization. While various ERM frameworks exist, such as the COSO ERM framework, ISO 31000, and the NIST Cybersecurity Framework, they share common elements and principles. Key components of ERM frameworks include:

Risk Governance: ERM frameworks establish risk governance structures, roles, and responsibilities to oversee and coordinate risk management activities across the organization. Effective risk governance ensures that risk management practices are aligned with organizational objectives, values, and risk appetite.

Risk Identification: ERM frameworks facilitate the identification of risks by providing methodologies, tools, and processes for systematically capturing and documenting risks across all business functions, processes, and activities. Risk identification involves engaging stakeholders, conducting risk assessments, and leveraging internal and external sources of risk intelligence.

Risk Assessment: ERM frameworks enable organizations to assess risks quantitatively and qualitatively by evaluating the likelihood and impact of risks on organizational objectives, performance, and stakeholder interests. Risk assessment methodologies, such as risk matrices, scenario analyses, and key risk indicators (KRIs), help organizations prioritize risks based on their significance and urgency.

Risk Mitigation: ERM frameworks support the development and implementation of risk mitigation strategies, controls, and action plans to reduce the likelihood and severity of adverse events. Risk mitigation measures may include process improvements, contingency planning, insurance coverage, hedging strategies, and technology solutions.

Risk Monitoring and Reporting: ERM frameworks establish mechanisms for monitoring and reporting risks, control effectiveness, and risk mitigation progress over time. Regular risk monitoring, key risk indicators (KRIs), control self-assessments (CSAs), and risk reporting enable organizations to identify emerging risks, control deficiencies, and areas requiring remediation.

Best Practices in ERM:

Effective implementation of ERM requires organizations to adopt best practices that align with their unique risk profiles, business objectives, and organizational culture. Some best practices in ERM include:

Leadership Commitment: Senior leadership's commitment to ERM is critical for fostering a risk-aware culture and integrating risk management into organizational decision-making processes. Executive sponsorship and support demonstrate the importance of risk management and empower employees to embrace risk management practices.

Stakeholder Engagement: ERM frameworks encourage stakeholder engagement and collaboration to ensure that diverse perspectives, insights, and experiences are considered in risk identification, assessment, and mitigation processes. Engaging stakeholders fosters transparency, accountability, and buy-in for risk management initiatives.

Integration with Business Processes: ERM should be integrated seamlessly into organizational business processes, strategic planning, and performance management systems to ensure that risk management practices are embedded in day-to-day operations. Integration with business processes enhances risk visibility, accountability, and effectiveness.

Continuous Improvement: ERM is an iterative process that requires continuous improvement and adaptation to changing risk landscapes, business environments, and stakeholder expectations. Organizations should regularly review and update ERM frameworks, methodologies, and practices to address emerging risks and enhance risk management effectiveness.

Technology Enablement: Leveraging technology solutions, such as risk management software, analytics tools, and data visualization platforms, can enhance ERM capabilities by enabling automation, data integration, and real-time risk monitoring. Technology enablement improves risk visibility, decision-making, and efficiency in ERM processes.

Conclusion:

Enterprise Risk Management (ERM) frameworks provide organizations with structured methodologies, tools, and best practices for managing risks systematically and proactively across the enterprise. By adopting ERM frameworks and best practices, organizations can enhance risk management effectiveness, resilience, and value creation. ERM enables organizations to identify, assess, mitigate, and monitor risks holistically, aligning risk management practices with business objectives, governance structures, and stakeholder expectations. In today's dynamic and uncertain business environment, ERM is essential for organizations to navigate risks, seize opportunities, and achieve sustainable growth. In the chapters to come, we will explore advanced ERM techniques, emerging trends, and case studies illustrating successful ERM implementations across various industries and sectors.

Chapter: Role of Technology and Data Analytics in Enhancing Risk Management Capabilities

In today's digital age, technology and data analytics play a crucial role in enhancing risk management capabilities for organizations across various industries. Advanced technologies and analytical tools enable organizations to identify, assess, mitigate, and monitor risks more effectively and efficiently, thereby improving decision-making, operational efficiency, and resilience. In this chapter, we explore the role of technology and data analytics in enhancing risk management capabilities.

Technological Advancements in Risk Management:

Technological advancements have transformed the landscape of risk management, providing organizations with innovative tools and solutions to address complex and dynamic risk challenges. Some key technological advancements in risk management include:

Risk Management Software: Specialized risk management software platforms offer comprehensive solutions for risk identification, assessment, mitigation, and monitoring. These platforms streamline risk management processes, centralize risk data and documentation, automate risk assessments, and generate real-time risk reports and dashboards for stakeholders.

Artificial Intelligence (AI) and Machine Learning (ML): AI and ML algorithms enable organizations to analyze vast amounts of data, identify patterns, trends, and anomalies, and predict future risks and opportunities. AI-powered risk management solutions enhance risk modeling, scenario analysis, fraud detection, and decision-making capabilities, allowing organizations to proactively manage risks and seize opportunities.

Big Data Analytics: Big data analytics tools enable organizations to collect, process, and analyze large volumes of structured and unstructured data from internal and external sources to gain actionable insights into risk exposures, vulnerabilities, and opportunities. Big data analytics enhance risk identification, assessment, and monitoring capabilities, enabling organizations to make data-driven decisions and optimize risk management strategies.

Cybersecurity Solutions: With the increasing frequency and sophistication of cyber threats, cybersecurity solutions play a critical role in protecting organizations against cyber risks and data breaches. Advanced cybersecurity technologies, such as intrusion detection systems, threat intelligence platforms, and behavioral analytics, help organizations detect, prevent, and respond to cyber threats effectively, safeguarding sensitive data and critical assets.

Cloud Computing: Cloud computing technologies offer scalable and cost-effective solutions for storing, processing, and accessing risk-related data and applications. Cloud-based risk management platforms enable organizations to leverage flexible infrastructure, real-time collaboration, and remote access capabilities, enhancing agility, resilience, and business continuity in risk management operations.

Benefits of Technology and Data Analytics in Risk Management:

The integration of technology and data analytics into risk management processes offers several benefits for organizations, including:

Improved Risk Visibility: Technology and data analytics provide organizations with enhanced visibility into risks by aggregating, analyzing, and visualizing risk-related data from multiple sources. Improved risk visibility enables organizations to identify emerging risks, assess risk interdependencies, and prioritize risk mitigation efforts more effectively.

Enhanced Decision-Making: Technology and data analytics empower organizations to make data-driven decisions by providing actionable insights into risk exposures, trends, and correlations. Advanced analytics techniques, such as predictive modeling, scenario analysis, and risk simulations, enable organizations to evaluate risk-reward trade-offs and optimize decision-making processes.

Increased Operational Efficiency: Technology-enabled risk management solutions streamline risk management processes, automate routine tasks, and reduce manual efforts, leading to increased operational efficiency and cost savings. Automated risk assessments, real-time monitoring, and workflow automation improve productivity and enable organizations to allocate resources more efficiently.

Proactive Risk Management: Technology and data analytics enable organizations to adopt a proactive approach to risk management by anticipating and mitigating risks before they materialize. Predictive analytics, early warning systems, and risk monitoring tools help organizations detect potential risks and vulnerabilities in real-time, enabling timely intervention and mitigation.

Enhanced Compliance and Reporting: Technology-enabled risk management solutions facilitate compliance with regulatory requirements, industry standards, and internal policies by providing robust audit trails, documentation, and reporting capabilities. Automated compliance checks, risk assessments, and regulatory reporting streamline compliance efforts and reduce the risk of non-compliance penalties.

Conclusion:

Technology and data analytics are integral components of modern risk management practices, enabling organizations to enhance risk management capabilities, improve decision-making, and achieve operational excellence. By leveraging advanced technologies and analytical tools, organizations can gain better visibility into risks, make informed decisions, and proactively manage risks in today's complex and interconnected business environment. In the chapters to come, we will explore advanced applications of technology and data analytics in risk management, emerging trends, and best practices for leveraging technology to mitigate risks and create value.

Chapter: Building a Culture of Risk-Awareness and Resilience

Building a culture of risk-awareness and resilience is essential for organizations to navigate uncertainties, seize opportunities, and achieve sustainable success in today's dynamic and complex business environment. A risk-aware culture fosters proactive risk management practices, encourages open communication, and empowers employees to identify, assess, and mitigate risks effectively. In this chapter, we explore strategies for building a culture of risk-awareness and resilience within organizations.

Leadership Commitment:
Establishing a risk-aware culture starts with strong leadership commitment and support for risk management initiatives. Senior leaders should demonstrate a proactive approach to risk management, communicate the importance of risk awareness, and integrate risk management into strategic decision-making processes. By setting the tone from the top, leaders create a foundation for building a risk-aware culture and fostering accountability for risk management across all levels of the organization.

Clear Communication:
Effective communication is essential for building a culture of risk-awareness and resilience. Organizations should promote open and transparent communication channels where employees feel comfortable discussing risks, raising concerns, and sharing insights. Regular risk awareness training, town hall meetings, and communication campaigns can help educate employees about the importance of risk management and empower them to play an active role in identifying and addressing risks.

Empowering Employees:
Empowering employees to take ownership of risk management fosters a culture of accountability and resilience. Organizations should provide employees with the necessary training, tools, and resources to understand and manage risks within their areas of responsibility. Encouraging collaboration, cross-functional teamwork, and knowledge sharing enables employees to leverage diverse perspectives and expertise in identifying and mitigating risks effectively.

Recognition and Rewards:

Recognizing and rewarding behaviors that contribute to a risk-aware culture reinforces desired attitudes and behaviors among employees. Organizations should acknowledge individuals and teams who demonstrate proactive risk management practices, take initiative in identifying and addressing risks, and contribute to enhancing organizational resilience. By incentivizing risk-aware behavior, organizations encourage a culture of continuous improvement and innovation in risk management.

Embedding Risk Management in Processes:
Integrating risk management into organizational processes, systems, and workflows reinforces a culture of risk-awareness and resilience. Organizations should embed risk management practices into strategic planning, project management, performance evaluation, and decision-making processes to ensure that risks are considered systematically and proactively addressed. By making risk management an integral part of everyday operations, organizations enhance their ability to anticipate and respond to risks effectively.

Learning from Mistakes:
Encouraging a culture of learning from mistakes promotes continuous improvement and resilience in risk management practices. Organizations should foster a blame-free environment where employees feel comfortable sharing lessons learned from past mistakes, near misses, and incidents. Conducting post-mortem reviews, root cause analyses, and corrective action planning enables organizations to identify systemic issues, implement preventive measures, and strengthen risk management processes.

Conclusion:

Building a culture of risk-awareness and resilience is essential for organizations to thrive in today's volatile and uncertain business environment. By fostering leadership commitment, promoting clear communication, empowering employees, recognizing, and rewarding risk-aware behavior, embedding risk management in processes, and learning from mistakes, organizations can create a culture that values proactive risk management practices and embraces opportunities for growth and innovation. In the chapters to come, we will explore case studies, best practices, and emerging trends in building a culture of risk-awareness and resilience across various industries and sectors.

FINAL THOUGHTS

In conclusion, building a culture of risk-awareness and resilience is not just a strategic imperative but a foundational element for organizations aiming to thrive in today's dynamic and uncertain business landscape. By fostering leadership commitment, promoting open communication, empowering employees, recognizing risk-aware behavior, embedding risk management in processes, and learning from mistakes, organizations can create a culture that values proactive risk management practices and embraces opportunities for growth and innovation.

As organizations continue to face evolving risks and challenges, cultivating a strong risk-aware culture will be essential for driving sustainable success and achieving strategic objectives. By embracing a culture of risk-awareness and resilience, organizations can enhance their ability to anticipate and respond to risks effectively, seize opportunities, and create long-term value for stakeholders.

In the journey towards building a risk-aware culture, continuous improvement, adaptability, and a commitment to learning will be key. By embracing these principles and leveraging the strategies outlined in this book, organizations can foster a culture that not only mitigates risks but also cultivates a mindset of agility, innovation, and resilience in the face of uncertainty.

www.ingramcontent.com/pod-product-compliance
Lightning Source LLC
Chambersburg PA
CBHW052207220526
45471CB00004B/1853